THESE MINOR MONUMENTS

THESE MINOR MONUMENTS

Fresh lights on china appreciation

CECILIA WOLSELEY

and

FELICIA SCHUSTER

ARCO PUBLISHING COMPANY, INC.

New York

First published in 1971 in the United States by
ARCO PUBLISHING COMPANY, INC.
219 Park Avenue South, New York, N.Y. 10003
Library of Congress Catalog Number 70–134273
ISBN 0–668–02408–9

© 1970 by Cecilia Wolseley and Felicia Schuster

Drawings by Robert Wilson

Printed in Great Britain

1560235

"Time, which antiquates antiquities, and hath an art to make dust of all things, hath yet spared these minor monuments."

SIR THOMAS BROWNE

Contents

CONTENTS

Preface

In preparing this little book and doing the fascinating research necessary to the writing of it, we felt that the reader would perhaps be more interested in the collecting of porcelain if he knew something of the men who made it, the factories where it was produced and the great attraction that it had for some notable personalities of the period when it was all the craze. Therefore, though we have tried to guide him in identifying objects for forming his collection and also to give him some idea of current market prices and the wares which are obtainable, we have invited him to step aside with us now and then to catch a glimpse, say, of Dr Johnson baking his own clay in the pottery at Chelsea, or the Rockingham potters sending the dinner service ordered by King William IV off to Windsor escorted by a squadron of cavalry, or again, Louis XV being forced by Mme de Pompadour to unpack the Sèvres porcelain with his own hands.

The porcelain-lover, taking a china bowl into his hands today, may feel a certain thrill when he thinks of a Mr Thomas Croft who, speaking of an eighteenth-century bowl made at Bow, says: "I had it in my hands at different times about three months; almost two weeks of my time was bestowed upon it." For this reason we have written about those factories which supply the most entertaining and revealing anecdotes and information, even though there are other factories of equal interest and value to the collector.

The pride taken by the craftsmen in their work, the delight in the making of a beautiful thing for its own sake, is largely what appeals to lovers of porcelain today. Even those who have no direct desire to invest or to collect may be interested in seeing these exquisite objects in museums or private collections, or in studying the beautifully illustrated books that are published about them.

We have included some examples and illustrations of objects which are not easily obtainable nowadays, although these rarities do occasionally, as we have tried to show, turn up in junk-shops and street markets. Some of the pieces illustrated in the photographs were picked up recently in shops and at markets, and for interest we have given their purchase prices as an approximation of their current value.

Though we have dealt primarily with English ceramics, many of the objects described have found their way to other parts of the world, such as the Liverpool mugs designed for the American market or the nineteenth-century figures of great poets and statesmen which are to be seen in many Commonwealth homes.

We have hesitated to deal with marks, as many of these are known to be unreliable. Smaller factories used to copy the marks of the great factories in the hope that their wares would sell better. An example of this is the Caughley copying of the Worcester marks. Even the great factories were not above such a deception, as, for instance, Duesbury of Derby who copied the Chelsea red anchor mark. We would therefore advise our readers, when buying porcelain, to rely on their knowledge of glaze and pattern, and only to concern themselves with the marking when these pointers seem to indicate that the object is of early origin.

This book is intended merely to open the door a little way on to the fascinating study of ceramics. If it succeeds in encouraging the reader to push the door wider for a fuller view of "These Minor Monuments", it will have achieved its aim.

Foreword

by Patrick W. Montague-Smith
Editor of Debrett

My cousins Cecilia Wolseley and Felicia Schuster have asked me to write a foreword to this book, explaining how it came to be written.

Cecilia has been writing and broadcasting on porcelain and allied subjects in England for several years. She has been on the guest-panel of the BBC's "Going for a Song", and has occasionally taken parties round many historic country houses. People are continually asking her to help them to identify their treasures, or to aid them in their collecting.

Collecting is obviously in Cecilia's blood. Her ancestor, Sir William Wolseley, 5th Baronet of Wolseley, roamed the Continent to amass *objets d'art*. She also has a family connection with the Wedgwoods.

Felicia, for her part, writes a weekly column on cultural subjects for a Paris magazine, and her father, Sir Victor Schuster, was an ardent collector of antiques. With the encouragement of their friends and Cecilia's audiences, they have written what they hope will prove to be an informative and, at the same time, entertaining book for the small collector.

Chelsea

RARE AND "BROKEN SUGAR"

The famous ceramic authority, Llewellynn Jewitt, tells us that "Chelsea is known for buns, pensioners and porcelain". We know all about the other two but, as Jewitt goes on to inform us, "fog obscures the beginnings of Chelsea". Through the mist we can see, around 1742, a Frenchman, Thomas Briand, exhibiting, before the Royal Society, specimens of fine white ware which, when broken, look like "broken sugar". Next on the scene, looming very large against the background of Lawrence Street and Justice Walk, appears a silversmith from Flanders, Nicolas Sprimont. Born in Liège in 1716, this *émigré*, both artist and craftsman, entered his mark as a silversmith in 1742 but, anticipating the mid-eighteenth-century craze for porcelain, he felt compelled to try his hand in the new medium. At first the paste was milky and translucent and the glaze soft and marked with a triangle. The first-known object was a goat-and-bee jug, dated 1745. The vessel, now in the Victoria and Albert Museum, London, sits on the back of two reclining goats with a bee in the front and a spray of flowers in applied relief. It is plain white, with the flowers picked out in colours, and has a handle in the form of a branch.

Sprimont's reign was short but successful. A writer of the period says that "under Mr Sprimont, the china was of such repute that it was purchased as soon as it was baked, dealers surrounding the doors for the purpose". All the dealers in London were struggling to get hold of it; thus we find a Mr Hughes, an ironmonger of Pall Mall, writing that he "has a greater choice of Chelsea Porcelain bought cheap and can be sold more reasonably than by the manufacturers themselves".

Sprimont's enthusiasm for porcelain, this fairy-like substance, was shared by many of the crowned heads of Europe, including Louis XV of France, and the Kings of Prussia and Naples. But at home the famous Dr Johnson went one further and actually turned his own hand to the making of it. He applied to the directors of Chelsea, who allowed him to bake his own mixture. We can imagine him going to the factory twice a week for the whole day with his housekeeper, who took provisions in a basket. Unfortunately this effort went unrewarded: the mixture came to pieces in the ovens. But the Doctor, though greatly disappointed, refused to alter his formulas.

Chelsea did not neglect to honour its poets. On its impressive shelves we find a figure of Milton, 11 inches (14 cm) high, with this inscription:

> Into the Heaven of Heavens, I have presumed, an earthly guest

and one of Shakespeare, of similar height, surrounded by his books, with the well-known quotation:

> The cloud-capp'd towers, the gorgeous palaces . . .

This conception of Shakespeare does not seem to have appealed to Pope, for he remarked that Shakespeare was represented as a "sentimental dandy".

The factory, however, went in for simplicity rather than for their usual grandeur when they launched out into reproductions from Aesop's Fables on table-ware. These consisted of red-brown rocks, blue and pink mountains, and lions with double-tufted tails. These modest little animals were painted with great economy of colour, the foxes, for instance, were almost completely red. Some of the animals which are in the Victoria and Albert Museum have lumpy joints and are arthritic-looking beasts with red tongues sticking out, as they are supposed to be continuously conversing.

Although the life of the factory was so brief it is interesting, as we stroll around Chelsea today, to pause a moment at Sloane Square and think of the man, Sir Hans Sloane, who gave the square its name. Sir Hans was a good friend to the Chelsea factory, putting his botanical gardens in Chelsea at its disposal, so that the painters were able to copy from nature. Some of these painters were the gentry of the factory, and in their own way were as distinguished as any Royal Academicians. They were allowed to give free rein to their artistic temperament, and more than a suggestion of the Latin Quarter was sometimes apparent in their dress.

Even more fantastic than the fantasies of the painters were the exquisite "toys" for which Chelsea was famed: scent bottles, seals, patch-boxes, *bonbonnières*, and so on. Luckily, eighteenth-century ladies used to carry their scent bottles in shagreen cases, otherwise these fragile but beautiful trifles might not have survived for us to see. One such scent bottle had a dog sitting on it, inscribed *Fidèle*. An eighteenth-century cynic points out that they had to stress the word *fidèle* (faithful) because that was the one quality noticeably lacking in those times. *Cosi Fan Tutte!* These little bottles often carried inscriptions in incorrect French on them, the reason being that the English craftsmen imagined French to be the true language of love. Thus two doves, billing together as stoppers, are saying, "*Imite-nous,*" and a monkey appearing from the front and the head of another with a clown's cap bears the caption: "*Je vous charmeiay*"; but they seem to have got it right with the infant Bacchus, "*Le vin, ami de l'amour*".

[3]

In spite of increasing fame and all the favours showered upon him, we find Sprimont describing himself rather curiously as an "undertaker of china-making" and petitioning the government to save him from unfair smuggling of Dresden china which, owing to an Embassy racket, was evading Customs duty and being offered for sale to Sprimont's customers. No attention, however, seems to have been paid to his complaints. This disappointment, together with his failing health and rising costs of production, finally induced him in 1769 to sell the business to James Cox, who only owned it for one short year before passing it on, in his turn, to William Duesbury. It had been a triumphant but brief reign, although the consistency of the china came in for its share of criticism, hence the nickname, "Broken Sugar". Baron Hill, an eccentric poet of the period, wrote: "Let any good workman in the potter's profession who would benefit himself by this art employ some poor people to buy up the old broken china which every house can afford him." Robert Dossie, a contemporary writer, in his book *The Handmaid to the Arts*, described the composition as "having almost the texture of glass, and consequently to break or crack if boiling water be suddenly poured on it". Perhaps this is the reason why so few pieces of this precious "Broken Sugar" are left to find their way into collectors' cabinets today.

A pair of Chelsea figures, 10½in/26·5cm and 9¼in/23·5cm

Left: Nineteenth-century Royal
Crown Derby basket
(£7; US $16

Below: Bow coffee can, about
1765 (£7·50; US $18)
Photos: Teresa Fairchild

Bow

PRECIOUS—TO BE KEPT WITH CARE

In a comedy of the mid-eighteenth century, entitled *Sir Courtly*, by John Crowne, we find the following lines:

> China, like women, should be kept with care,
> One flaw debases it to common ware.

Bow, though hardier than Chelsea and some other eighteenth-century porcelain, because of the calcined bones in the paste, has still not been kept with enough care to be anything other than a museum or a collector's piece. As Addison observed: "Some of them pay half their servant's wages in china fragments which their carelessness has produced." However, leave a little space in your cabinet, for though you cannot hope to own one of the famous Bow figures, a little trifle like a knife handle might come your way from the once famous "China Row" on the Essex side of the River Lea.

It all began when a young man called Frye travelled from Dublin to London to seek his fortune. Before Dick Whittington and after, many young men have done just this, but Frye, apart from being an excellent craftsman and artist, happened to be endowed with the vision that makes for success. He sensed that porcelain was in the air: all the world was talking porcelain. Thus Pope expresses the general feeling in "Lines Addressed to a Lady":

> Spleen, vapours or smallpox, above them all,
> And Mistress of herself *tho' china fall*.

B

[5]

Far from falling in Frye's capable hands, china was elevated to a new pedestal. This enterprising young man, with his wheedling tongue, soon managed to find a backer, one Edward Heylyn, who owned a glass factory at Bow, in London. Heylyn gave him a good start and by 1749 when Heylyn himself left the factory, substantial City men were easily found to replace him. Mr Weatherby and John Crowther, merchants of some repute, were both Freemen of the City of London and adopted a dagger from the City's coat of arms as their mark. In 1750 a new factory was built called New Canton, and by 1751 the annual sale of porcelain had reached £10,000—an unusually high figure for those days.

The first mention we have of Bow is in a paper in 1757: "If they can work to undersell the foreign porcelain, it may become a very profitable business to the undertakers, and save great sums to the public which are annually sent abroad for this commodity." The *Public Advertiser* tells us of "a large assortment of china for the use of Gentlemen's kitchens, private families and taverns"; while the Bow figures are advertised as "Gentlemen and Ladies 9/- each; Fiddlers, Shepherds and Shepherdesses, Columbines and Harlequins all nearly as cheap. . .". This "profitable business", unfortunately, came to an end for Frye in 1759, when he was forced to leave Bow, owing to failing health. It may have been about Frye that Goldsmith wrote: "There the pale artist plies his sickly trade."

The most flourishing period of Bow was from 1750 to 1762. Writing about Bow china, Horace Walpole says, "China collecting is a complete education"; and the porcelain craze has been summed up in these lines:

China's the passion of his soul,
A cup, a plate, a dish, a bowl
Can kindle wishes in his breast,
Inflame with joy, or break his rest.

This seems to have been true of a Mr Thomas Croft, who tells us: "This bowl was made at the Bow China Manufactury in 1760, and was much esteemed by the Duke of Argyll. I had it in my hands at different times about three months; almost two weeks of my time was bestowed upon it."

It must have been difficult to choose between such attractive china as that of Bow and Chelsea, but by and large Chelsea appealed to the nobility and the rich merchants, whereas Bow was more popular with the man in the street.

Like Chelsea, Bow prided itself upon its figure work. The early figures were imperfect and clumsily modelled, crudely coloured, yet full of strong, vigorous life. There is a clearness of outline, the result of use by a repairer of a sharp knife upon the folds of drapery and outlines of limbs. The garments are exquisitely pencilled with flowers, in bright and rich colours. Bow boys and girls look very much alike, except that the girl has a broad plait and the boy a cluster of curls. Bonny boys and girls, a little different from those of Chelsea, which are sturdier. Bow also made a figure of Mrs Clive, an actress of the period, in her role of Mrs Riot, who "lies in bed all morning, rattles about all day and sits up all night. She goes everywhere, and sees everything, knows everybody and loves nobody. She tells fibs, *buys china*, makes mischief, cheats at cards, keeps a pug dog, hates parsons, ridicules her friends and coquets with her lovers." Mrs Clive was not the only stage figure to be modelled; Garrick posed for Bow as Richard II, and Quin as Falstaff.

Through Bow we learn of an unusual musical instrument, a pastorella (modelled with the figure of a woman playing it), which was in general use before the introduction of the spinet.

As well as figures the Bow artists went in for birds, which they copied from nature rather than creating the exotic birds popular with other factories. They chose birds which were naturally colourful, such as cock-pheasants.

In spite of all this splendid enterprise the factory fell into decline, for in 1762 Weatherby died and in 1764 Crowther, his partner, was declared bankrupt. Fighting against heavy odds, however, he managed to carry on till 1775, when he was forced to sell out to Duesbury. Thus Bow was assimilated into Derby.

Sèvres

"HEADS, I WIN!"

If swindlers got their deserts, the Sèvres porcelain which enchants the world even today might never have sprung into being.

The Dubois brothers, run-away workmen from Chantilly in 1730, persuaded Orry de Fulvi, whose brother was the Comptroller-General of Finance, to set up a porcelain factory, asserting that they knew the Chantilly trade secret. Orry believed the brothers and gave them workshops in the kitchen-quarters of the Chateau de Vincennes. But though they may have been in possession of the secret, the experiments of the Dubois' were unsuccessful (five-sixths of their work having to be thrown away), and backer No. 1, King Louis XV himself, lost some 10,000 francs in the enterprise, until one day, as the story goes, a man named François Gravant made the brothers drunk and thus extracted the precious secret from them. But the work of the Dubois brothers was done. In 1745 they were dismissed, along with Orry's brother, who was replaced by a cultured and enlightened man named Machault. Under his control the business prospered; artists and chemists joined it, and the King's interest became so great that from this time onwards it was understood that the factory belonged to him.

In 1753 the King's favourite, Mme de Pompadour, suggested that the factory be moved to Sèvres, thereby bringing off a property deal of her own. Having got her "business" going, Mme de Pompadour was not slow in making hay while the royal sun shone. She received His Majesty in a conservatory where she was surrounded by flowers made out of Sèvres porcelain: tulips, lilies, daffodils, roses, etc., all life-size and coloured after nature; each separate flower perfumed with its own scent to heighten the illusion. A long way off from her beginning in life as a contractor's daughter! But commerce must have been in her blood, for never was business run more on a "Heads, I win! Tails, you lose!" basis. Courtiers were compelled to attend Court at Versailles; to absent themselves amounted to *lèse majesté* and could result in banishment or confiscation of estates. Once at Court, they would be buttonholed by Mme de Pompadour, who would remark pointedly that "to have money and not to buy porcelain is to prove oneself a bad citizen". She also saw to it that, by royal edicts, rival porcelain factories were limited to one pale colour and no gilding, whereas the Sèvres objects flashed with all the colours of the rainbow and were brilliantly gilded.

The factory demanded a very high standard of work. Many specimens were rejected and should have been smashed, or sold undecorated. But owing to procrastination, doubtful specimens were allowed to hang about, tempting the workmen to take them home illegally and paint them up; and thus began a series of clever forgeries that scarcely anyone but the greatest expert can spot, even to this day.

Mme de Pompadour's commercial instincts were sometimes side-tracked by the gaieties of Court life, so dull jobs like accountancy got shelved. Rich customers such as Catherine of Russia, for instance, begged to send small sums on account, after being supplied with substantial orders! No one employed in the factories seemed to be able to add or subtract, let alone make the necessary effort at pricing. All specimens of similar shape cost the same, regardless of the quality of the decoration. So it was "first come, first served". There was also a fantastic hold-up of delivery, especially in the department of figure-modelling, for which Sèvres had become world-famous. Instead of being carefully graded and stacked after use, the moulds were thrown together in a heap. One old workman, alone, could be relied on to find the mould that was needed; if he happened to be away, there was chaos. It is no wonder that, owing to these inefficient methods, finances were sometimes low, but Mme de Pompadour was no fair-weather friend to her factory. When things were difficult she opened a showroom in the Rue de la Monnaie, and sold buttons and artificial teeth. Moreover, she even succeeded in finding an active role for the King. As the dealers were afraid of the risks involved in handling the fragile porcelain, she made her royal lover open an auction-room and unpack the precious pieces with his own hands.

A business associated solely with royalty was naturally unpopular with the people, and the unpopularity reached its height during the reign of Louis XVI. The rich courtesans had their coaches decorated in Sèvres porcelain, and Marie-Antoinette not only had Sèvres porcelain plaques in her furniture, but when she was playing at being a shepherdess in her "Hameau" at Versailles, the dairy-churns and butter-dishes that she used were also of Sèvres. It is not astonishing, therefore, that when the Revolution broke out, the Sèvres factory was almost on the point of collapse, even though the director sold his own jewellery to pay the workmen's wages and pleaded with the Government to give them flour and meat to keep them going. In return for these favours the workers decorated the porcelain with tri-coloured borders and smashed the busts of royal personages and aristocrats.

Sèvres porcelain only regained its supremacy after Napoleon's rise to power. He took over the factory and put it on the sound financial basis on which it has rested ever since. He also used its skill to make vainglorious designs with Egyptian symbols, anticipating his conquest of the Nile. He even had the nerve to send the Empress Josephine a whole service decorated in this style after their separation, but with her usual dignity she sent it back unopened.

Under the Bourbon Restoration orders flooded in, quality improved, and new colours were added to the famous eighteenth-century ground colours, such as *"rose pompadour"*, in honour of Mme de Pompadour, *"gros-bleu"* (a darkish blue), *"bleu tarquin"* (turquoise) and *"jaune jonquil"* (a clear yellow). Pieces with these colours are, of course, collectors' pieces, but some early eighteenth-century bargains are still to be found.

Of course, it's all a gamble, but perhaps you will be lucky in the toss and become the proud possessor of an object from this exotic factory. Then, indeed, it will be "Heads, you win!"

M eissen

STRAW INTO GOLD

Confidence tricks have always existed. In the eighteenth century princes were besieged by would-be alchemists announcing that they were able to make gold. The princes often gave these tricksters the benefit of the doubt, probably because no matter how rich they were, they always wished to be richer. The story of the alchemist Böttger might almost be a variation on the fairy-tale of Rumpelstiltskin. Böttger had failed to deliver the promised gold to his patron, Augustus the Strong of Saxony. Augustus had counted on this gold to satisfy his craving for the fabulous and rare Oriental hard-paste porcelain that every crowned head in Europe, from Louis XIV downwards, was then scrabbling for. The rumour goes that Augustus carried his mania to the point of swopping a whole regiment of cavalry for three Chinese vases.

Furious with disappointment at Böttger's deceit, Augustus had him flung into prison and sentenced to death. Then, like the dwarf in the fairy tale, but kindlier, a friend appeared. Von Tschimhausen was a Saxon nobleman, but he was also a skilled chemist, and managed to persuade Augustus to pardon Böttger on condition that he (Böttger) worked under him in his laboratory. Böttger had no choice but to agree, but nevertheless he considered himself ill-used and wrote over the laboratory, "God, our Creator, has turned a gold-maker into a potter." However, as it turned out, Von Tschimhausen

[13]

made his "gold" for him or its equivalent, for he helped Böttger to discover that Chinese porcelain was made of china clay and china stone—and, lo and behold! Augustus was the first ruler in Europe to produce a hard-paste porcelain equal to that of the Chinese. Böttger's life was saved, and the great factory of Meissen sprang into being.

The factory opened near Dresden in 1711 and was an instantaneous success. Orders flowed in from all over Europe, custom being encouraged by the extreme courtesy of Augustus. Many stories are told about this as, for instance, that when the Sultan of Turkey placed an order, Augustus politely took off the mark of his own factory (crossed swords, which were a Christian symbol) and replaced it by Islamic symbols.

The most famous of all the Meissen modellers was Johann Kändler. He joined the factory in 1731 and served it devotedly until the day of his death. Kändler originally specialized in animals, modelling his birds from the stuffed ones in the Natural History Collection at Dresden. These were four feet high, and made for Augustus's Japanese Palace. But an amusing incident led Kändler to try his hand at figure-modelling. At Augustus's banquets the sugar ornaments down the middle of the table were apt to melt in the heat of the candles, so Kändler, to please his patron, invented figures in porcelain to replace those made of sugar. Once embarked on figure-modelling, Kändler's rather cruel sense of humour got the better of him. It was noted that the monkey musicians which he modelled all had the faces of the Dresden State Orchestra. Also, perceiving that one of Augustus's jesters was terrified of mice, he immediately made a figure of him with a mouse in his mouth! In his famous models of the Commedia dell'arte, his harlequin was known as the "indiscreet harlequin". He was, however, a little kinder to Augustus's mistress,

[14]

Countess von Cosel, who liked to call herself the "Pompadour de Saxe", and became the heroine of his crinoline groups.

Kändler worked harmoniously with another famous modeller, Christian Friedrich Herold, who joined the factory in 1725. Herold's work was in complete contrast with Kändler's. He specialized in landscapes with pretty little scenes of children at play, and flower paintings. He had his own methods of disguising slight imperfections in the kilns by painting small insects onto the objects. People admired these insects so much, however, that what had been meant to gloss over failures came to be a recognized part of Meissen decoration.

Kändler's able organization left him plenty of time for thinking out his fantasies. He had working under him no less than forty painters, twenty-five associates, eleven apprentices and two colour-grinders; and to keep up the social tone, he invited young noblemen "fallen into distress" to work in the factory, which they could do without losing face, as its reputation was so high. But working for Meissen wasn't all prestige. "Secret to death" was the legend written over the doors. It was indeed an offence punishable by death to leave the factory even at night or to divulge the secrets of the kilns. These secrets were faithfully kept until the Seven Years War, when Meissen was occupied by Prussian troops; several workmen then escaped to Vienna and to Berlin, taking the secrets with them. As a result of this war, production ceased, and Meissen lost its supremacy to Sèvres.

How are the mighty fallen! After the war the Meissen bagmen travelled Europe in vain; they came back with empty order-books. Various attempts were made to regain the factory's former glory during the Marcolini period (1774–1814), but lacking creative modellers, such as Kändler and Herold, Meissen could only copy old styles. There was worse to come. A second occupation during the Napoleonic Wars and competition from Wedgwood saw the factory in a truly sorry state after the Congress of Vienna. A debased revival of eighteenth-century rococo style, such as cherubs playing musical instruments, during the Kühn period, was hardly likely to improve matters. A merrier tone crept in in 1870 with the *Neuzeit* (new period) with contemporary girls in the bloomers they dressed in for bathing. This pre-heralded the *jugend-stil* (youth-style), better known as *l'art nouveau*, which sported maidens' legs, complete with stockings and shoes.

How would Augustus, who had been ready to sacrifice his kingdom for his factory, have reacted to this flippancy? However, by this time, Meissen was no longer Meissen; after the Napoleonic Wars it was referred to as "Dresden china".

Bristol

MOCK-CHINA

A new tax! Not if the Bristol glass manufacturers had anything to do with it! Clear glass was taxable under the Glass Excise Act of 1745, but the law left a loophole about opaque glass, so opaque glass it was for these "mock china" merchants. It was never intended to look like other glass, the aim was that it should be mistaken for porcelain. Painted in bright colours more beautiful than nature, this opaque glass became all the rage because Bristol was so near the fashionable spa of Bath. A Bath drawing-room of the period might have contained bottles and many beautiful varieties of vases, even cream-jugs and sugar-bowls, in this startling new fashion, but you would have looked in vain for a humble cup and saucer. The glassmakers disdained to waste their skill upon such objects.

These glassmakers of the middle of the eighteenth century took themselves extremely seriously; from early times glassmakers appear to have held a special position in Bristol. When the Prince and Princess of Wales came to visit the city, the Company of Glassmen led the procession on horseback, dressed in white holland shirts, some with swords, others with crowns and sceptres made of glass. They were so proud of their profession that we find one speaking of his engagement in a local paper and describing himself a "*glassman* about to marry a Miss Keinton". Indeed so highly did they prize their wares that when in 1763 a thief stole a pomatum pot with enamel flowers on it, they were more upset because he had forgotten to steal the lid than they were about the loss of what he did steal. Proud as they might be, they were not, however, above imitating Chinese porcelain designs, to which the opaque white background of the glass particularly lent itself. These designs were not an exact copy of Chinese art, but were a Western version, making up an imaginary Utopian land of gardens and flowering cherry-trees, of bridges and pergolas and distant mountains. Distance is said to lend enchantment, and as China was so far away that it was out of reach for most people, it became the Land of Heart's Desire. The *objets d'art* decorated in this style are known as *chinoiseries*.

One copy from the Chinese of elongated Chinese ladies carrying sunshades and towering over little boys was known by the curious name of a "Long Eliza". First made in the decorating shops of Canton such figures were called *Mei-Yen* or "Graceful Ladies", for the Chinese women, being short, liked to think of themselves as tall. But the Dutch merchants and sea-captains who brought these wares to Europe nicknamed them *Lange Lijsen*, literally "Long Stupids"; the nearest that English seamen could get to this, however, was "Long Elizas".

The Bristol glassmakers also copied designs taken from Chinese *famille rose* themes. The distinguishing feature of this work is a unique opaque rose-pink. In this the Chinese potters had, for once, borrowed a decorative idea from Europe. The colour was produced about 1650 from gold-chloride and tin by Andreas Cassius of Leyden and called "purple of Cassius". The Chinese called it *Yang Ts-ai*, or "foreign colour". Whilst carrying on this exchange of ideas with the East, Bristol traders seem to have clung to their native principles of honesty. They did not overprice their wares. In fact we find in one advertisement this admission: "The cheapness of Soppers Waste-Ashes enables us to sell our bottles cheaply."

The Bristol ladies, Elizabeth Anne and Martha Baker, when they set up their sign "At the China Jar" in Lombard Street, brought a similar honesty to London, for they announced simply that they sold "the best at the lowest price"—a statement which really happened to be true. But the sea-captains sometimes found it hard to live up to this high standard of integrity. A certain amount of smuggling of tea and brandy was carried on in the parcels of Bristol glass which they took to foreign ports in order to supplement their incomes, or possibly as presents to girls in return for favours received.

The solid burghers who were the hard core of the glass trade were soon to be treated to the mixed blessing of having a bird of paradise in their midst. Michael Edkins, who arrived in Bristol in 1760, combined his glass-painting with singing at Covent Garden. There is a limit to the output of any glass-painter, and it is doubtful if Michael Edkins painted all that is attributed to him, especially as he seems to have had plenty of time to make himself agreeable in society. An obituary notice tells us that "His uniform affability and urbanity rendered him equally esteemed in life as lamented in death".

Mocking china was not the only art of the Bristol glassmakers. The "Blue Bristol", for which they were also famous, refers to a colour of glass inclining towards violet rather than blue, and not, as may be thought, to the name of the city itself. Perhaps the most outstanding of Bristol blue objects were the decanters which had the name of the drink they contained in gilding upon them, in a festooned cartouche, so that it was impossible to hang a chain round the neck of the wrong decanter. One wonders if the son of an eighteenth-century father had once committed this crime, before the bottles were gilded. We can imagine that papa would probably not have been very pleased to find he had poured himself out a glass of "shrub" (a mixture of spirit, fruit-juice and sugar) instead of his sacred brandy!

[19]

With an unselfishness rare amongst craftsmen, the Bristol glass-makers took their special secrets of glassmaking far afield, into such regions as Lancashire and Ireland. Though, unfortunately, no Bristol glass is made nowadays, the large quantity of unmarked specimens which have survived keep their fresh colours as a testimony to the modest but superb craftsmanship of their creators.

Chamberlain Worcester plate, 1820, diameter 10in/25cm
(£4; US $10)

Above: Worcester Japan pattern cup, late eighteenth century,
2½in/6·5cm high (£8·50; US $20); and a Meissen boy with
birds, eighteenth century, 4½in/11·5cm

Below: Meissen candlestick, 6in/15cm; and an English Delftware
vase, nineteenth century, 3¾in/9·5cm (£5; US $12)

Derby

ANOTHER DERBY WINNER!

Imagine Derby Day on Epsom Downs without gipsies! In their gaily coloured costumes and gleaming earrings, threading in and out of the crowd, they give as colourful an effect as the deep blue and tomato china with which the wealthy ones amongst them invariably decorate their caravans. They may not always give sure tips for the races, but they have certainly backed a winner, themselves, in Derby porcelain. For these colourful pieces owe their origins to a Midlander, William Duesbury who, with his partner, Planché, founded the Derby factory in the middle of the eighteenth century.

Duesbury was born in 1725, and as a youngster worked as an outside decorator in London. A shrewd business man, he soon became the English porcelain tycoon of the period. His early porcelain was, however, very different from that of the Royal Crown Derby admired by the gipsies. It was glossy and chalky, white, very thinly glazed and clear and free from blemish.

From the beginning, competition to work for the factory was keen. In answer to an advertisement of Duesbury's, one applicant stated that he could give "unconscionable proof of ability and character" of which he was willing "to give ocular demonstration". As well as serious painting there seems to have been a good deal of junketing in these early days. The *Derby Mercury* reported: "The

C

body of a workman from the China Works missing on Christmas Eve, did not turn up till January 26th", and the painter Banford, whose wife took over his brush when he was tiddly, writes to his employer with a drunkard's remorse: "A slave to vice is certainly in a worse state than an African slave".

As well as having to cope with temperamental painters at home, Duesbury found time to open a salesroom in Covent Garden in 1763, and by 1769 his business was going ahead in such a dynamic fashion that he was able to take over the Chelsea factory and, along with it, many famous painters. 1770 saw the beginning of the great Chelsea-Derby period: decoration on table-ware, ground colours such as claret and turquoise, lapis lazuli blue, "Derby blue", festoons and swags, paintings of classical figures in grey and crimson, and Chinese landscapes with key-pattern borders. A rakish note was added to all this grandeur with the Derby birds, dishevelled-looking creatures in exotic colouring, with eyes an orangey-red that held in them a hint of the flirtatious.

Duesbury was a salesman *par excellence*, and he waited for the new moon and a brilliant assembly before presenting his goods for sale. In those days the "Quality" were renowned for their knowledge of fine furniture and exquisite porcelain, and the "sound of revelry by night" encouraged them further to exercise their talents as connoisseurs. Dr Johnson, himself, paid a visit to the Factory in 1777. Boswell describes his own reactions: "I admired the delicate art with which a man fashioned clay. I thought it as excellent as making good verse." But the Doctor found the china "too dear", and said he could have had vessels of silver as cheap. A nineteenth-century writer points out that Johnson, here, was probably wrong, because by that time this early eighteenth-century Derby was worth its weight in gold!

William Duesbury, himself, did not live to see this glorious era out; and it was his son's misfortune to have to cope with the continued threat of a Napoleonic invasion. Maybe the struggle that he had to keep the factory going hastened his end, for he survived his father by only ten years, and died before the victory of Trafalgar, which put an end to the danger of invasion. Keep the factory going he did, however, and after his death in 1796, it was carried on very capably by Kean, who had been a miniature painter in London before he came to Derby, and married Duesbury the Second's widow.

Thus the great era continued, aided by many famous painters, some of them slightly eccentric as, for instance, Quaker Pegg, who had a religious mania probably brought on by hearing Wesley preach, for he wrote to a friend at the time saying that "even Wesley had not enough of the Baptismal fire of the Holy Ghost". It is not surprising, therefore, that Peg considered it wrong to enjoy his own very skilled work and, denying himself the joys of creation, retired into a stocking factory, but even there he was worried about putting clocks on the cotton hose, thinking that they were too decorative. Luckily for Derby, the call of the artist was so strong within him that he returned to the factory for another eight or nine years of splendid work. The flowers that he painted were indeed little masterpieces, and can be easily identified because of their large size, but such was his modesty that very often he would write the name of the flower on the back, fearing that his skill at portrayal would not be sufficient for his customers to identify it otherwise.

Another eccentric was Hill, who rode to work on a pony called Bob. The pony carried his master along at a rapid rate, Hill sitting on his hindquarters with the long tails of his coat fluttering in the breeze, which earned him the nickname of "Flying painter" or "Jockey Hill".

Billingsley, one of the most competent of the painters, was apprenticed to Derby at seventeen. It was he who invented a new style of drawing roses from all aspects, even from the back. It was said of his flower paintings that "the weight of the flower produced a curve which one can fancy changing with the flutter of the breeze."

The dawning of the new century was to see many changes in ceramic history in which Derby, as one of the most important factories, should have taken the lead; but unfortunately Kean, although steady, was not a man to set the Thames on fire and in 1811 the factory was bought by Robert Bloor. Bloor's ownership, which lasted till 1846, was known as the "Bloor period", and was a disaster for Derby. Bloor provided a blatant example of honesty not always being the best policy. In his misplaced enthusiasm to pay off the Duesbury family in record time, he resorted to the mistake of touching up "seconds" (ie, discarded pieces). This would have been bad enough had the work been reasonably executed, but instead it was done in a slipshod manner. When, on top of this, Bloor lost his reason, the factory took a downhill plunge from which it never recovered. The year 1848 saw its close. The workmen dispersed, but a few, still loyal to their city, formed themselves into a company called Locker and Co., and so vaguely kept the flag flying. But Locker died in 1859 and although his successors, Stevenson and Hancock, made a gallant effort to carry on, the shutters went up for the time being. Fortunately for the gipsies, and for us, the new Derby Company which rose phoenix-like in 1876 had not only substantial financial backing but was to acquire a Royal Warrant from Queen Victoria in 1890, when it became known as the "Royal Crown Derby Company", under which title it remains today. The new company revived many of the old styles, and on the factory's nineteenth-century work the marking is more reliable than on that of the eighteenth-century: another aid to the gipsies, and to you, if you happen to be looking for a Royal Crown Derby piece.

Worcester

"THE FAITHFUL CITY"

Writing in 1878, Llewellynn Jewitt says of Worcester: "There are three things for which the Faithful City is celebrated: porcelain, gloves and sauce. For who has not drunk out of Worcester china, worn Dent's gloves or tasted Lea and Perrin's sauce?"

This is almost an echo of an earlier voice: "Dear sleepy old Worcester, city of loyalty, pottery and gloves." Both writers seem to have agreed upon the point of Worcester's faithfulness, which is certainly in no doubt if work has anything to do with it, for its factory has the longest history of any pottery in England. It was established in 1751, by a Dr John Wall and thirteen of his business associates. Apart from his profession as doctor, Wall was also a painter. He is described as being "never without a picture on his easel", and when a friend asked him how he had time to do all he did, he answered simply, "I make time."

He certainly made the chemists find time for experimenting in a new type of paste, by putting soap-stone in the kilns. "Who has not drunk out of Worcester china?" asks Jewitt. But why specially Worcester china? Well, in the eighteenth century, if you wanted to show off and silently announce that your china cupboard was so well stocked that you could afford to lose a cup or so, you never put the milk in the tea-cup first. To do so would have been tantamount to letting on to visitors that you hadn't much china to spare. Hence the rhyme:

[26]

May all your flowers die of thirst,
Your cutlets burn and éclairs burst
If you *will* put the milk in first.

Hostesses, therefore, to make a good impression, allowed the hot tea to damage the decoration on their tea-cups or even to break them, rather than lay themselves open to the charge of being poor. But with his addition of soap-stone to the paste, Dr Wall became the housewife's friend. How they must have blessed him when they read his announcement that he had "At cheap prices pieces that are not only very light but which have great tenacity, and bear hot water without more hazard than the true china ware". That his invention was wholeheartedly acclaimed we know, for we find him adding: "The nobility and gentry are desired to leave orders in time, as we have more to execute than can be performed. . . ."

Having thus got his factory off to a flying start, Dr Wall was not slow to follow up his success, but even he would have been surprised had he been able to foresee that the most famous of all the Worcester periods to which his name was attached was to be carried on seven years after his own death by a curious collectors' fiction. For though Dr Wall himself died in 1776, the work carried on by William Davis was still known as the "Wall Period" till 1783, seven years after his death.

Something must now be said about the style of this period. Early wares were often in the *famille verte* (Chinese), green, yellow, purple, over-glaze red and under-glaze blue, forming a five-colour palette. But the Worcester copies were not pure copies, because their colours were less lustrous and vivid than the Chinese. However, an eighteenth-century soft-paste copy of a *famille verte* can more than likely be attributed to the Worcester factory. As well as these highly-coloured wares, Worcester produced very large quantities of blue

[27]

and white, tall Chinese figures with long talon-like fingers, and many Japan patterns. From the first a distinguishing quality of Worcester was a colour that was greyish or blueish in tone, when held up to the light. This was due to a touch of cobalt, expressly added to counteract the yellow hue so disapproved of by the eighteenth-century collector with his enthusiasm for the pure white paste of the Far East. A pleasant little touch of snobbery! Landscapes appeared around 1770, and so did heavily painted fruit. The year 1780 saw the beginning of the classical urge, and Grecian urns appeared with heavy blue borders. It is interesting also to note that noble families were in the habit of sending their crests to China, so that the Chinese could make up special services for them which were known as "Chinese armorial porcelain". Worcester cashed in on this fashion and began to make armorial porcelain sets themselves, the earliest known example of this being a rococo shield with the Tracy Arms in 1756.

One of the greatest strokes of luck that came the way of the factory during this Wall period was the arrival of Robert Hancock, following the closing down of the Battersea enamel factory. Hancock was at Worcester from 1757 to 1774, and is famous for being a pioneer of transfer-printing, ie, printing under the glaze by means of pieces of paper taken off copper-plates. He had learned at Battersea from the Frenchman Ravenet how to engrave delicate subjects from Watteau and Boucher. He did not go in for much original work as most of his subjects were copied from contemporary paintings and a magazine entitled *Ladies' Amusement*. Imagine Gainsborough, whose work he also copied, classed with the pictures in this magazine!

Hancock's earliest known work is a mug of the King of Prussia, described rather wordily by Thomas Carlyle: "There stands on this mantelpiece a small China mug, not a bad shape, declaring itself in some obscure corner to be made at Worcester, and exhibiting all round it a diligent potter's apotheosis of Frederick. It offers a poor, well-meant portrait labelled 'King of Prussia', twenty years too young for the time, smiling out nobly upon you, and from the top there descends a small Cupid, who has forgotten his bow, and tries to drop onto Frederick a wreath far too small to get on (his head). This tolerable china holds a good pint." On this mug, however, Carlyle had not said the last word, for a rhyme of the period runs:

> Beauty may triumph on a China Jar,
> And this perhaps with stronger faith to trust
> Than the stain'd canvas or the marble bust.

After William Davis's death in 1783, the fiction of the "Wall Period" ended. The factory was bought by the London agent, Thomas Flight, for his two sons, who were both in the jewellery trade. Flight senior confined his activities to the London side of the business, leaving the Worcester side to his sons. He seemed to understand London requirements better than his predecessors, and his influence led to a change of style, the neo-classical. The early patterns of this period were simple blue painted and printed flowers, with blue bands with or without sprigs, richly decorated with gold. One of their patterns, called "Blue Lily", was chosen by King George III for a breakfast-service. This same George III, when attending the Three Choirs Festival, rose early, saw the cathedral and walked over almost every part of the town before 7 a.m. Later, in the afternoon, he visited the premises of the factory, now Messrs Flight and Barr, saw the process of china-making and left ten pounds for the workmen. He admired the work so much that he advised Flight and Barr to open a showroom in London, which they did; and George himself, in 1788, gave Worcester a Royal Warrant.

[29]

Before this, in 1783, Chamberlain, a former Worcester associate, left the employ of Worcester and started a rival business in the same city, endeavouring to meet public taste rather than to improve it. His efforts seem, anyhow, to have been appreciated by Lord Nelson, who visited the Chamberlain works with Lady Hamilton in 1802 and declared that "not even at Dresden [Meissen] have I seen anything better". An authority of the period, however, tells us that Chamberlain wares were so completely covered with patterns as to hide all minor defects. Indeed, when in 1840 an amalgamation finally took place between Chamberlain and Worcester, it was known as a *mariage de convenance* and not of love—not very surprising seeing that the rival proprietors had been conducting their business on such different principles.

One of the better-known painters of the Flight and Barr Period, which lasted from 1783 to 1840, was Baxter, who joined the factory in 1815. An amusing anecdote is told of him. The great musician, Mr Hope, invited Baxter to see his collection of china, saying that in England there were no artists as good as the French. Hope then took up a piece of china and said, "I bought this in Paris." Whereupon Baxter replied, "I have seen this plate before." "Oh, no," said Hope, "that is impossible." "I have not only seen this plate before," said Baxter, "but I have painted it myself." This was proved to be true.

After the Chamberlain Period, the business was taken over by Kerr and Binns, from 1852 to 1862. The best-known painter during this period was Bott, of whom it was said that, "Gradually undertaking higher and higher flights, it would seem as though, the zenith of his art being attained, there was nothing left for him to reach, for soon after these vases were completed, he passed quietly away."

"Higher flights" seem to have been the hallmark of this period, for the factory even attempted to illustrate Shakespeare's *A Midsummer Night's Dream* on a dinner-service, going so far as to suggest what was passing in the mind of the poet. Thus the designs include a figure of Shakespeare sleeping on a bank, with fairy heads protruding from branches above his own, indicating how his thoughts are forming.

After 1862, the factory became known as the Royal Worcester Porcelain Company—a name which it still holds today. Today, also, it is still possible to find a little Dr Wall "Blue and White" for a few pounds. The much later Victorian Worcester, which is also attainable, shows the influence of Persian, Italian and Indian styles. In the late Victorian period there are some attractive jugs, tea-pots, etc., in the form of leaves, and buff-and-cream ivory vases, priced at about £1.50 (US $4) a piece.

A visit to the "Faithful City" and a tour round the works will give a fillip to the interest of any would-be collector.

Liverpool

THE CUSTOMER IS ALWAYS RIGHT

After it had won the War of Independence, the young American nation naturally felt that it wanted to stretch its wings and trade with Europe. So, westward bound, its ships took the port of Liverpool on their way. Was Napoleon so wrong in calling the English "a nation of shopkeepers"? The Liverpool porcelain makers certainly put business first. They did not hesitate to reproduce portraits of the American conquerors on their mugs, to be eagerly purchased by American sea-captains and their crews. The customer is always right!

Who were these Liverpool porcelain makers? The first one we hear of is Robert Podmore who, arriving from Worcester in 1750, entered into an agreement with Richard Chaffers of Liverpool and Philip Christian, another Liverpool potter. Podmore was to supply the knowledge and his partners the capital. Porcelain was also made in the city by some smaller firms who followed Podmore's lead so blindly that they were said to be "Podmorizing". These manufacturers were so bound up in their own work that during the election campaign of 1761 their song ran:

> Regardless of great ones, we live uncontrolled,
> We're potters and plumbers, we are not to be sold,
> No purchase but merit can cheapen such souls,
> Thus circled in Friendship we live by our bowls.

It was a sad blow to the Liverpool porcelain industry when Podmore and Chaffers both died prematurely of fever in 1765. Their work, however, did not die and was carried on successfully by one of the smaller firms, James and John Pennington, until 1780. After this the industry deteriorated and, in spite of the efforts of the youngest of the Penningtons, Seth, porcelain making finally ceased in 1805.

Some wares are obtainable nowadays, from the period 1755–65, usually known as the Chaffers Period. Chaffers was so famous for mixing colours that Wedgwood said of him, "This puts an end to the battle [of trade]. Chaffers beats us all in his colours. He can make colours for two guineas which I cannot produce so good for five." On these early wares the potting is thin and neat, the paste has a green translucency and the glaze is thin. Podmore, for his part, had brought the styles of Worcester with him. The Liverpool exotic birds, however, differ from those of Worcester. These birds have plump, rounded contours, are crested and spotted, with yellow necks, green and blue wings, red bodies, and rumps under which the tail-feathers are coiled in a becomingly coy manner. They are remarkable birds and can be found perched on red, twiggy branches with dark-green leaves like those of fig-trees. There are also the Liver-Birds, emblematic creatures copied from the city's arms, where they flap their bronze wings grotesquely on the top of the Royal Liver Building.

A speciality of the factory was the "marbled blue", where the colour is veined with gold to produce a marbled effect.

A design unique to Liverpool is a gnarled tree. Instead of being called by their names, the painters were known as the "dab" artist, or "spiky-flower", "jointed branch" or "knotted-tree" painter. The last-named painted trees which had almost bare branches, as in

[33]

winter. Blue and white was made during all periods, but printing only began in 1765 in heavy, wet-looking dark-blue, also in black. In the printing the river scenes have impossible fishermen with incredible equipment. There are also Chinese garden scenes, with for instance a Chinaman beckoning to a flock of birds.

The bulk of Liverpool porcelain was made for domestic use by simple people. Therefore the objects to look for are chamber-candlesticks, snuff-boxes, cornucopias and pickle-trays, chimney ornaments, etc. It must be remembered, also, that Liverpool being a sea-port, boats and ships played a great part in its porcelain decoration. We may still find today bowls with names of ships made to commemorate the termination of a successful whaling or slave-taking venture, illustrating, at the same time, the history of Liverpool.

John Robinson, who worked for Seth Pennington, had the audacity to paint on a bowl, "Success to the African Trade", so we see that Wedgwood was more than justified in his fight against African slavery. Occasionally, in their designs for America, the potters exercised a sense of humour: "Success to the crooked but interesting town of Boston,"—to remind Bostonians that they had by no means overcome their town-planning problems.

Though the Liverpool porcelain industry ended more than a century before World War I, it anticipated a famous character of that war, for on one of its mugs is portrayed an elderly man with a walrus moustache, who might be the prototype of "Ole Bill" of 1914–18, himself.

Wedgwood

NOT ALL LAVENDER AND WHITE

The name of Wedgwood is apt to conjure up a picture of those lavender-mauve objects, decorated with white reliefs, figures, garlands, festoons, etc., that one often sees nowadays. But these graceful and dainty creations, to many people Wedgwood's signature tune, do not by any means cover the full scope of his genius. Wedgwood, in fact, undertook the creation of pieces in his kilns the like of which no potter had ever attempted before. There was his black basalt (Egyptian black) with its rich smooth surface, decorated with unglazed colours in imitation of ancient Greek vases. There was his "rosso-antico", a red-ware of extraordinary beauty. There was, also, his cream-ware, subsequently called "Queensware", because in 1762 he had given Queen Charlotte a breakfast-service, and in 1765 the Queen allowed him to describe himself as "Potter to her Majesty". This ware was mostly plain or sparsely decorated and it relied for its success on symmetry of form. Finally, there was his jasper-ware, the lavender-and-white which we know so well, sometimes varied with subtler colours of blue, green, lilac, pink and yellow. There are two types of jasper-ware: the solid, which is coloured throughout, and jasper-dip which came in later and was used for more delicate effects, where the colour was only on the outside.

Josiah Wedgwood's pottery started in 1759 in a modest way, at

Ivy House, Burslem. He was immediately successful, because unlike some of his more unfortunate contemporaries, he possessed a business sense equal to his talents. One might say that, like King Midas, everything he touched turned to gold. An avant-garde of the neo-classical craze, his wares were instantaneously successful, and it is no exaggeration to say that he became a rich man almost overnight. It has been said that "Pope translated Homer into English verse, and Wedgwood translated classic designs into English pottery".

No amount of success seems to have been able to spoil this lovable man. Mr D. Darwin writes about him: "I never knew of a man raising himself to such opulence and distinction who excited so little envy." His purse was always open to those in need, and his sympathies with the under-dog made him an ardent supporter of anti-slavery. He never bore any malice, even refusing to sue for debts, and going so far as to stop proceedings and pay all costs if he found any of his subordinates doing so. He detested keeping accounts and said that he would rather lose thousands than enter upon the details of figures. Once, to please his wife, he tried to keep accounts on a journey. He entered the first item of expenditure, a penny he gave to a girl for gathering flowers, but found himself unable to continue because he began immediately to meditate upon colours.

He was also immensely hospitable. His home, Etruria Hall, was more like a first-class hotel than a country house, so numerous were his guests. But although his house was so full, he always had more places than there were visitors laid at the dinner-table, in case friends should turn up unexpectedly. What his cook thought of this enthusiastic hospitality we do not know, but she was consoled by being given moulds specially designed by the factory in the classical styles, for her jellies and desserts.

Nor did Wedgwood-ware shine only upon English tables. In 1774,

Nineteenth-century Wedgwood jug, 4¾in/12cm high
(£5; US$12)

Jug by Christian's factories, Liverpool, 3½in/8·5cm high
(£14; US$34)

Worcester armorial cup, nineteenth century, 2½in/6cm high

Caughley bowl, eighteenth century, 1¾in/4·5cm high
(£2.50; US $6)

no less a personage than Catherine II of Russia, styled by Wedgwood in his rather prim way, "The Messalina of the North", ordered a dinner-service from the firm. The service was called *La Grenouillère*, meaning marsh-place full of frogs, because Catherine wanted it for her Palace La Grenouillère, outside St Petersburg, and it was therefore duly decorated with a whimsy of small frogs. It was painted in brownish-purple with a border of mauve flowers, and the centres represented 1,200 different scenes of Britain. When this impressive service was exhibited in London in Greek Street, Soho, it caused quite a sensation amongst the élite.

It may seem surprising that Wedgwood, the thirteenth child of simple Staffordshire potters, could have fallen so easily under classical inspiration, and what is more, knew how to adapt its art to modern requirements. For this we must thank Bentley, whom Wedgwood met in 1762 and who remained his partner until his (Bentley's) death in 1780. Bentley was a classical scholar and guided his young protégé towards a love of the classics. Wedgwood, an apt pupil, obligingly put classical figures all over his jasper-ware, but he never exaggerated to the extent that some sculptors did when they dressed up the statue of George Canning, which stands in Westminster Abbey, in a toga. Wedgwood, however, seems to have had some doubt whether he should go all the way with the classicists, for we find him writing to his chief modeller Flaxman: "The nude is so general in the works of the Ancients that it would be very difficult to avoid the introduction of naked figures", though in early Victorian times, his successors, mindful of public reaction, were careful to drape these figures a bit more thoroughly. Rather surprisingly, however, even in Wedgwood's day we find a figure of Jean-Jacques Rousseau clad in Armenian costume and Voltaire, of all people, in a blue cloak, terra-cotta coat and lilac vest. Public events,

D

[37]

also, such as the fall of the Bastille, lent new inspiration to Wedgwood and he invited a friend's opinion as to whether it would be indelicate to put the heads of aristocrats on the top of snuff-boxes!

The two partners, Wedgwood and Bentley, usually saw eye to eye, and they were also born craftsmen. For instance, on the day when they opened their works "Etruria", they both took part in the actual potting, Wedgwood announcing that "Work consecrates the hand which does it".

These new works enabled Wedgwood to increase his output to include many small, inconspicuous items. Had you seen a fashionable lady and gentleman strolling about in those days, they might have been unconscious walking advertisements for this well-publicized business. The heels of the lady's shoes, her hair-pins, rings, cameos, earrings, medallions and châtelaines, as well as the gentleman's walking-stick handle and fob-chain, would, as likely as not, have been made by Wedgwood. The gardens of these same ladies and gentlemen were decorated with Wedgwood orange-tubs, basket-pots and rustic holders for young bulbs, whilst their houses contained wainscots, doors, pilasters, and plaques inlaid in the furniture.

Wedgwood also made figures of famous American personalities, such as Lafayette and Benjamin Franklin, for the growing American market, but his opinion of these "settlers" was slightly patronizing. He considered that England was the father and America the child. "We have driven out the brat in his infancy, and reposed him in an uncultured forest, to the mercy of wild beasts and savages."

This upright and estimable man was not without his little foibles, including a tinge of slight snobbery. In his letters he constantly refers to "titled visitors": "It seems that a vase madness is breaking out among titled folk. The Duke of Leinster was in raptures. . . .". He also commissioned artistic society ladies, such as Lady Diana

[38]

Beauclerk and Lady Templeton, to draw him charming little domestic scenes with, of all things, infant bacchanalia!

Perhaps, on the whole, his life has been well summed up by the engraving on his tombstone at the parish church of Stoke-on-Trent: "He converted a rude and inconsiderable manufactory into an elegant art."

Swansea and Nantgarw

"YOUR INFANT MANUFACTORY"

"I am happy in receiving your pottery . . .". Thus did Lord Nelson encourage the efforts of the Welsh potters. "And," continued his Lordship, "I hope that its being used by *me* may be of service to your Infant Manufactory."

The Welsh manufactories in earthenware and later in porcelain of Nantgarw and Swansea may have seemed like infants compared to the commercial English giants of Worcester and Derby, but they had the courage in the early nineteenth century to produce soft-paste wares that were serious rivals of the Sèvres *pâte tendre* of the eighteenth century—a feat which the eighteenth-century manufacturers for all their skill, had been unable to achieve. The same paste was used at Nantgarw and Swansea: a bone-ash variety, containing china clay and a glassy frit, or soft paste. No paste, even the finest soft paste of Sèvres, has a purer, whiter translucency, devoid of all cloudiness.

The leading light in this enterprise was the famous rolling-stone of porcelain, no other than our old friend Billingsley. Having failed to settle at Derby, Worcester and other smaller factories, Billingsley, with his son-in-law, Samuel Walker, and his two daughters, turned up in Nantgarw. As always impecunious, he was determined to make an impossibly expensive porcelain, though his contemporary manufacturers were content with serviceable, adequately decorated wares.

[40]

Fortune, it is said, favours the brave, and soon a financier, William Young, appeared. But his help, though timely, was not sufficient because of the ruinous kiln-losses incurred in making so expensive a paste. Ever optimistic, Billingsley did not hesitate, with the help of an investigator called Dillwyn, to petition the Government for financial assistance. The attempt failed, but Dillwyn, who owned the Swansea Cambrian Pottery, invited Billingsley and his son-in-law to make their porcelain at Swansea. This was in 1814, but unluckily for this venture Worcester, to whom Billingsley and Walker were still under contract, intervened. Legal proceedings were started and in 1816 Dillwyn was obliged to ask them to leave. They went back to Nantgarw and struggled against heavy odds till 1819, when the factory was forced to close down.

Nevertheless, this "infant manufactory" had achieved a remarkable output for its short history, of which three-quarters of its wares were plates and dishes and the rest small decorative pieces, such as spill-vases, candlesticks, tankards, pen-trays, etc. A writer of the period states: "The ware was so beautiful, as many as forty gentlemen's carriages had been known to be there in one day." The wares may have been beautiful and also expensive to make, but they were by no means cheap to buy. Thus: "When you feel your purse is too heavy, you take it to Mortlock's [London agents] in Oxford Street and tell him that you are panting for ice-pails of Swansea china." Regardless of the expense, many strangers came from a distance to purchase the wares, and the more respectable inhabitants of Swansea were also eager customers. A famous Welsh bard, whose name was Iola Morganwg (in English, Edward Williams), wrote to the Rev. David-Davies of Neath, in London: "Before leaving Cardiff I intend to see the porcelain of Nantgarw, supposed to be the finest in Europe, and superior to the French. I have seen articles of it as white as snow." No less a personage than Turner visited Swansea and some plates were engraved after his work by a painter named Rothwell.

There were a number of talented painters employed in the factory. One, Thomas Pardoe, who came to Nantgarw from Bristol, was known for painting large pink roses, fully opened and multi-petalled —roses so life-like that they put one in mind of Thomas Moore's famous lines:

> You may break, you may shatter the vase if you will,
> But the scent of the roses will hang round it still.

Pardoe, like Pollard, another painter, was unsurpassed in the painting of wild flowers, anemones, pinks, fox-gloves, rust-coloured wall-flowers, forget-me-nots and celandines. He was particularly fond of deep purple and bright yellow, which he used whenever possible.

Since Billingsley had been in charge of the factory he had had less time for painting, but Henry Morris was able to imitate his style so well that it was difficult to tell the difference. Morris's talent for imitation earned him an unusual compliment. Dillwyn received from London a specimen bowl made at Sèvres and an order for a dozen similar bowls, and Morris executed the order. When the London merchant wrote asking for the return of the Sèvres bowl, it was explained to him that it was among the others. The London dealer was then forced to admit that he could not distinguish the original Sèvres bowl from the copies Morris had made.

Men painters were not the only ones to be employed by the factory. We learn that Hannah, a daughter of one of the executives, "painted much above the average for a painteress", and throughout all his chequered career, Billingsley had always been able to count upon the help of his two daughters, also "painteresses".

We can imagine Billingsley's feelings when his precious factory folded up, but, true professional that he was, he bravely went to Coalport and continued to work there until his death in 1828.

Caughley and Coalport

THE PLATE ON WHICH THE SUN NEVER SETS

The Willow-Pattern that we knew
In childhood with its bridge of blue . . .

had a habit of turning up in unexpected places, even, it is said, on half
a saucer supposed to have been picked up by a cardinal in the crater
of Vesuvius, probably in the late eighteenth century.

However this may be, it was in 1780 that Thomas Turner, the
proprietor of the Caughley porcelain works, launched this bit of
triumphant *chinoiserie* on the world.

Everyone knows the legend of the Willow Pattern plate. What
Turner did, in fact, was to invent a kind of Chinese Lord Ullin:

"Come back, come back," he cried in grief
  Across the stormy water,
"And I'll forgive your Highland Chief,
  My daughter, oh, my daughter!"

with his story of an angry Chinese father pursuing his eloping
daughter and her lover. The Chinese, themselves, were amazed to
find that they had become the subject of such a legend, as there is
no prototype of the Willow Pattern in Chinese ceramics. Turner's
flight of fancy, however, was eagerly sought after and dispatched to
English people in all parts of the globe, so that without exaggeration
one could say that there was no spot on the earth's surface where there
was no Willow Pattern. It was as frequently seen on cottage tables as

[44]

on those of the nobility. But as time went on it suffered many changes: the original birds became flying fish and the placid lake was transformed in a grotesque and strange fashion into wind-driven trees. Variations on the Willow Pattern are well worth looking for today.

Let us now take a look at Caughley (pronounced Calfley), where the Willow Pattern was launched. It was Thomas Turner, the inventor of the pattern, who introduced porcelain making to an already existing pottery at Caughley in 1772. Turner had learnt his business of potting at Worcester, so the early wares were similar to those of the Severn town. This factory, being one of the lesser lights of the eighteenth century, made numbers of small objects decorated in underglaze blue, which gives the minor collector today a wonderful opportunity of acquiring that rarity, a piece of eighteenth-century English soft-paste porcelain at a modest figure.

The most familiar patterns to look for are the pine-cones, parrot and fruit, copies of Worcester in fluted sauce-boats, cabbage leaves, moulded jugs with mask-lips, and small vases. There are various types of transfer-printing: conventional groups of flowers and fruit copied from Meissen; Oriental designs with or without figures; sprig-patterns after the manner of the French factories; and English figures and landscape subjects—apart from the famous Willow Pattern itself.

Though most of the designs were of a simple nature, the Caughley personnel were, according to a writer of the period, out to better themselves mentally. In the *Gentleman's Magazine* of 1777 John Randall, speaking of the death of a Caughley worker, says: "He served his time at Caughley, the earliest of our Shropshire porcelain works and the nursery of a class of clever men." Numbers of these "clever men" worked together in a room, one sometimes reading

[45]

aloud for the benefit of the others. The repartee was as lively as in the House of Commons; the rooms were nicely warmed and there was a woman appointed to bring coals and keep the tables clean. Men with these advantages rose to higher situations. Some became linguists, schoolmasters, engineers, etc. In such an environment it was only natural that the boss Turner himself should have been attracted to France, that centre of culture, and in 1780 we find him paying a visit to the French porcelain factories and bringing back French workers and French colours to Shropshire.

Turner's reign at Caughley lasted until 1799, when he sold the business to John Rose, who had a pottery at Coalport. Though Rose was to become very successful in the next century, he had an unlucky start, for when the River Severn overflowed its banks after the autumnal rains the ferry-boat, crowded with forty-one of the Coalport workers, capsized and twenty-eight of them were drowned. The *Shropshire Gazetteer*, reporting on the incident, said of Rose: "The generous master of those who perished provided coffins at his own expense for their internment, and was frequently seen to shed tears. His benevolent conduct towards the surviving sufferers will never be forgotten." Some of Rose's best craftsmen were lost in the tragedy.

After this unfortunate accident matters improved. John Rose was an excellent businessman and founded the good relationship with Sèvres which, much later in the 1850s, led to Coalport artists being sent to Sèvres, and to Sèvres actually sending moulds to Coalport for the use of the English factory. Coalport also mounted their vases in ormolu, as were the original Sèvres pieces. In 1820 the Society of Arts offered a prize to "the person who shall discover the cheapest, safest, most durable and most easily fusible composition without lead", for lead was causing workers' paralysis. This medal was won by Rose.

Turner's aspirations had been modest ones, but Coalport in the nineteenth century went in for elaborate painting, extravagant gilding and compositions of modelled flowers applied to riotous scroll-work. For the small collector, however, there is more homely Coalport to choose from, such as candlesticks, pot-pourri jars, and pastel-burners; table-ware, clock-cases and ink-stands; and night-lights in the form of cottages with masses of tiny flowers all over them, such as carnations and sweet-peas. All these are often to be met with today.

John Rose ran Caughley and his own factory at Coalport together for ten years, before moving Caughley over the river to join Coalport. This is why the whole concern then became known as Coalport, under which name it remains today.

Lowestoft

"A TRIFLE FROM LOWESTOFT"

Miracles do happen. Some Bow and Chelsea figures, rare as they are, have occasionally been discovered in an attic, but he for whom eighteenth-century china is "the passion of his soul" does not need a miracle of good luck to stumble across "a trifle from Lowestoft".

These "trifles" originated from one of the remotest corners of eastern England, on the Suffolk coast, where most of the inhabitants were engaged in the herring-fishery. In 1756, Hewlin Luson discovered clay on his estate and erected a small kiln. The story goes that the discovery was brought to Luson's notice by a grateful Dutch sailor whom he had saved from drowning. However, after this romantic beginning, the enterprise petered out, for the London porcelain manufacturers were jealous of even so remote a competition, and by subtle bribery they managed to stage a kind of eighteenth-century go-slow. Luson gave up; but in 1757 the business was revived by Messrs Walker, Browne, Aldred and Kickman. London again tried to bribe the workmen, but the new management was too strong for them. Browne himself must have been a man of extraordinary ingenuity, for, wishing to turn the tables on his competitors, he dressed himself up as a workman and got into the Bow works, where he learnt secrets which he brought back to his own factory. For this reason it is sometimes extremely difficult to tell the difference between wares from Bow and those from Lowestoft.

Browne died in 1771 and his son, Sir Robert Browne, carried on the business; but the factory came to an end in 1802, having fallen a victim to Napoleon's ruthless burning of English goods on the Continent, because, as well as the Lowestoft factory, the Brownes had unwisely invested in a warehouse in Rotterdam.

In spite of its brief history, Lowestoft managed to produce an astonishing number of objects. A great many of these were made for the people around, and the designs on them show a sense of simple rural fun. For instance, for a Mr Trulls, tobacco-merchant, the design was the figure of a man hoeing a tobacco-field. On a punch-bowl made for a ship called the *Judas*, there were pictures of the ship itself. Out of these bowls the crew drank to success before each fishing-voyage, and at carousels at the end. In 1768, Armond of Wymondham, proprietor of "The Rising Sun", was presented with flowers and a sun in splendour depicting a human face, on a mug; but it was with a Negro on his mug that Edward Jex, the owner of the Blackboy Inn at Beccles, was presented. This same Jex entertained King George II and gave him to drink out of his Lowestoft mug when his Majesty's ship was obliged to put in at Lowestoft for a few hours, owing to contrary winds on its way to London. A lady called Mary Cather was celebrated in rhyme:

> May love continue.
> And happiness increase,
> Live in love,
> And die in peace.

As was also a blacksmith:

> By hammer and hand,
> All Art doth stand.

Apart from these intensely personal objects, Lowestoft, being then a fashionable seaside resort, created a number of small and delightful wares, suitable for presents, such as eye-baths, feeding-cups, egg-cups, food-warmers, birthday plaques, and minute tea-services with which children could pretend their dolls were entertaining each other. Many of these objects had written on them, "A Trifle from Lowestoft", foreshadowing the vogue for Goss china at the end of the nineteenth century. Like the Lowestoft trifles Goss ware could only be purchased in the town whose Borough Arms appeared on the china object. Good business for both the borough and for Goss!

We will describe Lowestoft wares in some detail because, as we have suggested, there is still a good chance of finding pieces from this factory today.

The early ware was almost entirely underglaze blue, occasionally indigo in tone, the translucency being colourless, occasionally palely green. The tea-pots are globular with closed rosebuds on the lids, and the coffee-pots have scrolled handles. Chinese landscapes and simple arrangements of flowers are used in decoration; and after 1770, transfer-printing was introduced and became popular till 1785. Designs to look out for are coarse dark-blue flower and fruit patterns, or Chinese pagodas in a landscape, or sometimes vignettes of churches and views, as well as sporting-prints, such as a huntsman and dog, or a sportsman with a gun.

Tea-services and coffee-pots are numerous, but plates and dishes are rare. The larger plates have long spur-marks on the underside near the rim, and the blue painting is inky in tone, by contrast with the bright, neat painting of Bow.

In 1773 we find enamel colours used in conjunction with underglaze blue. From 1770 to 1780 mugs were made in three sizes with splendidly painted flower-sprays, especially tulips, but later, unfortunately, these gorgeous tulips disappear and a pattern from France, including cornflowers, takes their place.

The birthday plaques have two holes pierced near the rim for suspension. Names are in roman characters, and on the obverse side there are flowers, cottages, heraldic roses, figures, foxes and doves of peace.

Lowestoft traded with Turkey, but for that market no design of man or beast was permitted for fear of offending the Mohammedans; instead, a crescent was painted at the bottom of each piece.

A rose is a frequent emblem on Lowestoft porcelain in tribute to a French painter of that name, who came to the factory at the time of the French Revolution. But sadly enough this refugee, though he became old and blind in the service of the factory, was given a donkey as sole reward for his loyalty.

Lowestoft never had an official mark of its own but, flying high it imitated the marks of Chinese porcelain, Worcester and Meissen.

No one in their senses, however, would be deceived by such naïve trickery. In any case the delicacy and charm of its wares can stand on their own merits. A "trifle from Lowestoft" is an asset to any collector's cabinet.

Minton

"THE OLD SÈVRES DESIGN"

The journal of the Society of Arts said of Herbert Minton: "In an insular country such as England with a large and increasing population, it will probably be conceded that a man who creates any new industrial resources must be a natural benefactor."

Herbert Minton, who succeeded to his father's porcelain business in 1836, was the second in the line of this potting family of Stoke-on-Trent. A writer of the period describes him rather fulsomely: "Neither a man of profound research nor an educated artist, neither an economist nor an inventor, but by courage and ceaseless energy, he had this rare union of qualities on which are impressed the stamp of genius and win lasting honour for his memory."

Herbert Minton's "ceaseless energy" led him to become a pioneer of the English ceramic industry. He was nothing if not conscientious, going the round of his own workshops every day with his foreman. "William," he would say, "do you think this colour is too strong?" Or, "William, is there force enough in that figure?" Or again, "Do you think that if the decoration was extended a little more it would look better?" The result of all this forethought was that goods which until then had been exclusive to factories such as Chelsea, Bow, Worcester and Derby became objects of ordinary supply.

Addison once said: "China vessels are playthings for women of all

Staffordshire earthenware: a Punch children's plate (Allerton &
Sons, 1860). Diameter 5½in/14cm

Swansea and Nantgarw plate

Staffordshire willow pattern
plate, diameter 6in/15cm

ages. An old lady of fourscore shall be as busy cleaning an Indian Mandarin as her granddaughter is in dressing a baby." Minton was to bring glamorous wares within the reach of many such ladies, old and young. Not too delicate for ordinary use, either. On the occasion of an exhibition of English manufactures, one of Pickfords' van-men was delivering a load of china at the entrance, and as he dumped it carelessly on the floor, the official in charge grumbled at him, fearing damage. "Oh, never fear, sir," the man replied, "It's Minton's; it won't break." How unlike Chelsea's "broken sugar"!

The porcelain's beauty seems to have matched its solidity, for we are told by a writer in France during the French Exhibition of 1861 that "many people would award to Minton's as much credit as to Sèvres". The writer added: "It was a piece of good fortune to Mr Minton that both he and the Imperial Manufactory should exhibit at the same time vases of the old Sèvres design, because in some instances the advantages were on the side of the English Firm." No wonder that when the Duke of Wellington toured manufacturing districts with the Duke of Sutherland, he so admired the Minton porcelain that he ordered his carriages to stop, much to the delight of the workmen, who were eager to welcome the hero of Waterloo.

What were these wares like that were so appreciated by the Duke? They were decorated with flowers, birds and animals, landscapes and garlands, bouquets and *fêtes galantes*, framed in radiant backgrounds of blue, canary-yellow and turquoise. Unlike many of the "rarities" of eighteenth-century porcelain, many of these splendid examples from the Minton factory are not tantalizingly out of reach, but are obtainable today. Not long ago in London one of the authors found half a soap-dish in *rose pompadour*, which she uses for a rose-bowl,

E

for 25p (US 60 cents) at the Church Road, Edgware Road, Saturday street market.

Minton's did not confine its output to the more standardized types of porcelain. From the middle of the nineteenth century onwards it copied French faience (earthenware) and Italian maiolica wares. The faience gives an effect of intricate inlay, its pure white clay body being covered with interlacing arabesques, whose spaces are fitted with various coloured pastes. The factory also made pure white statuary ware called "Parian ware", something after the style of the famous Sèvres biscuit-ware of the eighteenth century. Once it had to apologize for being late in the delivery of some Parian ware: "We shall be sending you tomorrow one Madonna, but without a Crown, and we very much hope to have four Dorotheas by Saturday."

Tiles were also a speciality of the factory, but here Minton's did not always get the co-operation it needed. We find a newspaper remarking, "Our modern architects have singularly neglected to avail themselves of Mr Minton's beautiful revival [tiles], but the use of it at Paddington Station is unexampled".

Minton's one-time partner, Boyle, when working around 1840 for the factory, wrote to some American friends: "This manufactory is second to none, and embraces every kind of ware. We make many articles which no one else makes. The prices are high, but they are cheerfully paid." Boyle was probably referring to some of the more unusual types of Minton wares such as cheese-toasters, bee-hive shaped honey-pots, pickle-sets, oval butter-tubs, chamber-pots, soap-boxes, tooth-brush trays, and tea-strainers.

The wares ranged from the sublime to the ridiculous, and it was alluding to them that a contemporary quoted a seventeenth-century poet, Robert Wilde:

[54]

MINTON

Here lies a piece of Christ, a star in dust,
A vein in gold, a china dish that must
Be used in Heaven, when God shall feed the just.

Staffordshire

FIGURATIVELY SPEAKING

Among the Staffordshire potting figures, real or imaginary, there is perhaps none so popular as Sir Toby. Appearing in England in the middle of the eighteenth century, Sir Toby is the descendant of a long line of illustrious ancestors. Face jugs can be traced back as far as ancient Egypt, Babylon, Crete and Cyprus. The funny man of ancient Greece, Silenus, son of Pan, who acted as preceptor to the young Bacchus on certain Greek vases, is depicted lying asleep on a wine-skin. On Roman jugs there are painted faces of the god Mercury; and later in South America some jugs turned up that bear a marked resemblance to Tweedledum and Tweedledee. In medieval England knights used to wash their hands in face-jug ewers, and in the seventeenth century in Germany, an unpopular cardinal who persecuted Protestants appeared on their stone-ware jugs (called after him "Bellamines") as a caricature. The Toby jug, some hold, was probably made after a notorious Yorkshire tippler, who was reputed to have drunk £9,000 worth of Yorkshire stingo, or strong beer! Others think that it was based on another tippler, Henry Elwes, said to have put away no less than two thousand gallons of beer in his lifetime. Such prodigious feats of drinking were quite enough to conjure up a jug like Toby, but the truth is that he was inspired, of all unlikely countries, by Italy. He was copied from a popular engraving, published about 1761 to illustrate a song translated from the Italian by a clergyman named Francis Fawkes. The song runs:

> Dear Tom, this brown Jug that now foams with mild ale
> In which I will drink to sweet Nan of the Vale,
> Was once Toby Fillpot, a thirsty old soul
> As e'er drank a Bottle or fathom'd a Bowl . . .

So "Toby Fillpot", himself, was just an eighteenth-century attempt at punning!

Toby was joined by a band of cronies, a veritable *Comédie Humaine*, the thin man, the night-watchman, the sailor, the lawyer and many more, including Martha Gunn, the bathing-woman of Brighton, who was said to have dipped the infant Prince of Wales, later George IV, in the sea. There were often inscriptions on Toby jugs, such as: "Not for you, Boney!" And for cricketers: "It's all out, then fill it again!" Toby was still popular in Dickens's time, for in *Barnaby Rudge*, Gabriel Varden says to his daughter: "Dolly, put Toby this way, dear!"

The price of the Toby jug, which once could be seen frothing over with beer in every tavern, now reaches impressive sums in sale-rooms little dreamt of by the eighteenth-century "regulars", if made from the well-known Ralph Wood's work in coloured glazes. On the other hand, an ex-sailor of the authors' acquaintance, whose hobby it is to collect Toby's female cronies, managed to unearth the "Gin-Woman" for a few pounds in a junk-shop in Paddington. Modern Tobies can, of course, be obtained for the asking.

There was a nonconformist element among the Staffordshire potters which led to their making the Established Church of England their Aunt Sally. A vicar is depicted asleep in a wig in the pulpit, whilst the clerk sits underneath, exhorting the congregation; and some plasticine-looking figures, known as "pew-figures", can be seen with supercilious expressions on their faces, sitting in church porches surrounded by musical instruments and bottles of wine. Into this nonconformist stronghold came Voyez, a skilled modeller from France, and the inventor of the bucolic and convivial jug known as "Fair Hebe". This gay spark, in his cups, was imprudent enough to model in the half-nude the virtuous daughter of Wedgwood's coachman, much to Wedgwood's puritanical disgust.

An even more entertaining invention than Voyez's Hebe jug were the reversible-headed pots, which made effective play with contrasting characters, such as the Pope and the Devil:

> Think not the painter of this piece uncivil
> To delineate the features of a Devil,
> He means no more than carefully to trace
> The Pope's resemblance in th'infernal face.

The end of the eighteenth century also saw figures of pagan gods and goddesses, and rather prim young ladies wearing dresses enamelled with sprigs, which give them a slightly Jane Austenish touch.

The potters found it easier to model people than animals. Since there were no zoos in those days for them to copy from; it is not surprising that some of their animals look more like fabulous beasts than actual inhabitants of the jungle.

The nineteenth century saw the revival of real people in Staffordshire pottery: the royal family, leading politicians, actors and actresses, and poets; even murderers were not excluded. From America came Benjamin Franklin, George Washington and, waving the garment that made her fame, Mrs Bloomer in person.

Earthenware could also be a medium for world events, like the death of Nelson and the assassination of Marat, just as if the potters were producing illustrated magazines.

To satisfy the craving for horror innate in human nature, two potters, Obadiah Sherratt and his wife Martha, invented a kind of Chamber of Horrors of ceramics. Any event that took place in the far-flung British Empire was grist to the mill for this bloodthirsty pair. For instance, they modelled a tiger stalking off into the jungle with the head of a certain Lieutenant Monroe in its jaws, severed from the body, which trailed behind. An incident that was unfortunately taken from life!

Tamer animals were also to be found on the mantelpieces of many cottages, such as the sturdy poodles, rather sentimental-looking spaniels, and sporting dogs of all kinds.

The eighteenth-century Staffordshire figures fetch high prices, within the hundreds, today, but "Eminent Victorians" in this ware were made in such vast numbers that a few are still likely to be scattered about in junk-shops, and it is always possible that you may come upon the head of Gladstone peeping from behind a pile of old mattresses or even a commode.

Spode

BEWARE THE TIGER!

Although Josiah Spode gave his name to, and played an important part in the founding of, this famous factory, it is perhaps his son, Josiah Spode the Second, whose name will go down in ceramic history. He was not only the inventor of English bone china, but he was also responsible for drawing English attention to India and Asia Minor.

However, the part played by Josiah the First must not be underestimated. Apprenticed at sixteen to Whieldon, the most famous potter of his age, he left his master after five years to set up on his own, manufacturing blue and white china and coloured pottery, and in 1776 he himself became a master potter. In 1779 he found his ideal partner in William Copeland, a splendid salesman and manager, who ran the pottery in Lincoln's Inn Fields, leaving Josiah the First to look after the more inventive side of the business at Stoke-on-Trent. Josiah's taste was good; he managed to achieve splendour without vulgarity. Even before Japans became popular, he experimented with hybrid patterns in Oriental style, zig-zag fences and shrubs in blue, green, red, pink and gold. The fashioning was faultless and the gilding solid and rich. His fruit painters, who were usually anonymous, achieved a style at once realistic and inviting. The flower painters favoured full-blown bunches with one or more roses greater than life-size. His tea-services were painted with subjects from natural history. In general, his porcelain appealed more to the professional classes, lawyers, doctors, and rich merchants, than to the masses.

His son, Josiah Spode the Second, who was to bring the factory to fame, had the good fortune to learn the business both from his father and his extremely capable partner, Copeland. His invention of English bone china was a novel use of known ingredients and was copied by all the major nineteenth-century factories and those of the eighteenth century which survived, such as Worcester and Derby. Apart from bone china, Josiah the Second produced the best blue and white porcelain of his period. The pottery was good, the modelling extremely careful and in the printing the pictures were clear with no smudging, and the borders did not run over the edge. The colour of the blue varies slightly; some specimens are faint, others deeper. The glaze is silky and soft to the touch, and it is light in weight.

It seems only natural that the inventor of bone china should have had an active imagination; and Josiah the Second, the child of his age, which had been deeply interested in Rome and Greece since the excavations of Pompeii and Herculaneum, went even further than the archaeologists and Wedgwood and the Brothers Adam, reaching out towards India and Asia Minor. In those days before cameras, if manufacturers wanted to paint pictures on their china, they had to take them from illustrated books. It happened that a certain Captain Thomas Williamson published in 1805 a book entitled *Oriental Field Sports*. Owing to the scanty knowledge of India amongst English people, who perhaps imagined that their sons on foreign service were being devoured by jungle beasts, this book was an instantaneous success. Spode, who was nothing if not an opportunist, immediately reproduced the illustrations of these animal hunts on his porcelain.

The curious thing is that nobody seems to have thought of copying him; therefore the odd elephant or tiger on blue-and-white ware is a sure sign of genuine Spode.

It is interesting to examine some of Williamson's quotations, so aptly illustrated by Spode. No wonder the English public were apprehensive about what was going on in India when they read, for instance: "A tiger, when hard put-to for a meal, will often take away a young gentleman . . .", or wondered what their loved ones were going to look like when they did re-appear, for: "Sometimes an officer will bear upon him the marks of a leopard's fury"; or, if they were lucky enough to escape the tiger and the leopard, "The jackals possess such steady adherence to their purpose as in the end to over-come the small portion of care and vigilance usually to be found among the servants . . .".

Spode's imagination did not stop at India. Thus we find him reproducing illustrations from Georges Perrot's *History of Art in Phrygia*, where the contrast between Perrot's travel-tales and early nineteenth-century England no doubt afforded Spode some amuse-ment. Such as this: "The orgies of Dionysius offered stupendous opportunities for the portraiture of the human figure . . . The audacious attitude of the worshippers, men and women, whose conflicting passions, caused by wine and religious frenzy, were reflected in their whole being. Our practical everyday life has nothing which resembles the tumult and rebellion of the senses. The Greeks, in the palmiest days of their artistic existence, never lost their taste for the gross pleasures afforded by orgies."

Like all his contemporaries of the Regency period, Spode was ruin-minded and created porcelain with ancient Roman remains, such as the "Tiber Pattern", "Locarno Pattern" and "Blue Italian", as well as many others. But he could also bring his mind down to practicalities.

Some small inexpensive collector's gems are still to be found in knife-rests (knives were not removed with each course), strainers, soup and gravy ladles, etc., side by side with his more imposing subjects.

Doulton

THE HOME OF THE WOMEN ARTISTS

"We, the Lady Artists, desire to express our obligations to you for elevating so large a number of our sex. We also desire to record our very high appreciation for the arrangement made for our comfort."

Thus did the "Lady Artists" write in a volume, around the middle of the nineteenth century, which they presented to Henry Doulton, their employer, who was the first pottery manufacturer to encourage women to take a leading role in the creative side of his business. The best-known of these women was Hannah Barlow, who became internationally famous for her spirited drawings of animal subjects. When she lost the use of her right hand because of the dampness of the clay, she courageously learnt to draw almost as well with her left hand. Her work has been compared to that of Rosa Bonheur, the famous nineteenth-century animal painter.

Henry Doulton, this benefactor of women, was the son of the founder of the business who, judging by Dickens, was by no means so benevolent as Henry. "During this distressing period of my childhood," writes Dickens, "I had to paste labels on thousands of Doulton and Watts blacking-bottles." It is interesting to think that Doulton's, who started with bottles before pottery, should be the true name for the "Murdstone and Grinby" firm in *David Copperfield*. To the end of his life Dickens would look back on the misery of his bottle-blacking days. He seemed unable to rid his mind of the

[64]

humiliation, though Doulton's themselves had probably long forgotten that they had once employed the future literary genius of the
age as a bottle-blacker.

John Doulton, the founder of the firm, born in 1793, was apprenticed to Dwight, at Fulham, who was one of the most skilled potters
in London. By 1815 Doulton was able to establish his own business
in Vauxhall, and took as partner John Watts. When the Napoleonic
invasion was threatening, John Doulton expressed his views in
sentiments not unlike those of a Churchill: "It is difficult to conceive
the state of England at this juncture. The Nation's heart beats in grand
unison." John Doulton had higher aspirations for his son than that
he should be a potter; but the son, in spite of a university education and
his father's wish for him to become a lawyer, chose to go into the
business. Through a friendship with the local headmaster of the
Lambeth School of Art, whose name was Sparks, and who suggested
new forms for vases and jugs to be made at the Doulton works by
the Lambeth students, Sir Henry conceived the original notion of
giving these young people the run of his works. The students so
encouraged produced objects that attracted attention at the Paris
Exhibition of 1867, and also at the South Kensington Exhibition of
1871, which resulted in Sir Henry Doulton's being recognized by the
Society of Arts for impulse given to artistic pottery. No other potter
had ever been awarded this honour.

One of the specialities of the factory was Reform Law bottles
with heads of King William IV and Lord Grey, of which a contemporary writes that, "London gin tasted better when it emerged from
the top of the bewigged head of the Lord Chancellor." Doulton's
also made hunting-jugs, loving-cups, inkstands, faience dishes and
tiles, flower-pots and bed-warmers, most of them obtainable today.
An unusual product was the terracotta plaques of religious subjects in

churches; and there were also curious and comical animal groups engaged in human pursuits.

Doulton's caused a renaissance of salt-glazed decorated stoneware in England. It created its own tradition, independent of the salt-glaze of Staffordshire. Doulton's hand-made pottery spread all over the civilized world and led to the development of modern studio pottery. For this salt glaze different methods of decoration were used, such as dots and flowers. Wares consisted of warm yellow-brown and white-and-cream vases and jugs; candelabra, chessmen, clock-cases, oil-lamps and name-plates for houses. The factory did a humorous line in puzzle-jugs with several spouts that made it difficult to pour without spilling, causing much merriment to lookers-on. Nor did it forget the eighteenth-century favourite, Sir Toby, for it brought his prototype to life again in 1933 in many of Dickens's characters and others, such as Old Charlie, Parson Brown, Dick Turpin and even Winston Churchill himself, though these were models of head and shoulders only.

Little did the poor young boy Dickens, slaving away at Doulton and Watts, dream that one day this same Doulton would be modelling the characters from his novels.

Vienna

THE GRANDEUR THAT FADED

At the height of its triumph, after the conquest of the Turks, Vienna, at the beginning of the eighteenth century, built palaces that had not their equal in Europe. The splendid Italian decorated walls and ceilings called for the finest porcelain to offset them, so 1718 saw the beginning of the Vienna porcelain factory. A year earlier, in 1717, Hunger of Meissen had been persuaded by the Viennese Ambassador in Dresden to go to Vienna. Suitable raw materials were found nearby, and Du Pacquier started the business with Hunger, Zeider and Becker as partners. When this Du Pacquier, of Dutch origin, left his position as *Hofkriegsratagent* to the Court, the Emperor granted him a privilege to make porcelain; wisely, as it turned out, for the Du Pacquier period of Vienna porcelain has been described as producing "precious stones", so brilliant was the harmony of colour.

In the patent granted to Du Pacquier are these words: "This is no ordinary craft; it is a secret art." To keep your porcelain secrets in those days was not always easy. One factory, jealous of another, would do its best to lure outstanding workers away. Du Pacquier had already won the tug-of-war with Hunger, and this encouraged him to go on a talent-spotting expedition to Meissen and meet Stölzel, one-time kiln-master under Böttger. Du Pacquier approached Stölzel in a coffee-house and played billiards with him, deliberately allowing him to win. Gratified, Stölzel then agreed to come over to

Vienna for a thousand thalers a year and fringe benefits to include a carriage; but Stölzel gained little by his desertion, for the promised salary was not forthcoming, and another two years saw him back at Meissen again.

In spite of trying to steal each other's secrets, Meissen and Vienna kept their styles distinctive. This can be seen in Meissen's brilliantly gowned little Chinamen who look as if the artist were poking fun at them, whereas the Viennese Chinamen tend to be eclipsed by the landscape and foliage. But all the same Vienna had some *chinoiseries* in the form of dragons, though its dragon, like that of most Europeans, was erroneous from the Chinese angle. (The Chinese dragon is often a harmless and beneficent animal. It demands no tribute of virgins, it breathes no fire, and its habits are quite unlike those of the Western dragon.)

During the Du Pacquier period, most of the work was decorative. Very little table-ware was made because, Vienna having become an important artistic and cultural centre, the nobility were only content to eat from magnificent silver dishes.

Early wares of the Du Pacquier period bear a close resemblance to those of Böttger. They are decorated with leafy scrolls, coloured in purple, with iron-red *chinoiseries*. Landscapes containing figures were also produced in the style of Meissen. Shapes were often based on silver-ware of the period. The ware was usually unmarked before 1744; but these pieces are rarities today.

Even in those days the prices were so high that hardly anybody could afford to buy the wares. Rather than cheapen the splendour of his porcelain (his "precious stones"), Du Pacquier sold out to the Emperor, who generously allowed him to stay on as Director until his death in 1751. The factory grew in size, but the turnover still failed to offset the heavy State subsidies, until, in 1785, Von Sorgen-

Nineteenth-century lustreware jug, 4½in/11·5cm high
(£5; US $7)

Victorian china fairing, 5in/12·5cm high (approx £3·50; US $8);
and a nineteenth-century Coalport mug, 3in/7·5cm high

A bear potlid, diameter 3in/7·5cm (£30; US $72)

thal took charge and accounts immediately became healthier. The Von Sorgenthal Period (1784–1805) is considered by many to be the factory's finest. Von Sorgenthal did his best to raise the artistic level, refusing to take apprentices who had not passed drawing-schools. He also spared no expense in hiring the best artists to paint his china. A leading chemist, Leithner, was engaged to prepare colours and gilding and was successful in producing a new dark-blue ground and a red-brown which are distinctive marks of Vienna. Sorgenthal also produced china painted after the manner of Watteau and Boucher, and classical figures and topographical paintings. He shows a charming little human touch in the making of specially constructed cups and saucers, known as *trembleuses*, for elderly ladies whose shaky hands were liable to upset a normally shaped cup.

Until Von Sorgenthal took over the factory, the Viennese bourgeoisie had been in the habit of buying faience (earthenware) because they were unable to appreciate porcelain. To awaken their interest, Von Sorgenthal introduced State lotteries with porcelain prizes, which had the desired effect of increasing his clientèle.

On Von Sorgenthal's death in 1805, the factory was taken over by Niedermeyer, who brought the art of gilding to near perfection and kept the finances in good order. But under further directors the work declined, till by the middle of the nineteenth century, poor workmanship and lack of initiative proved such a burden on the State that it closed the factory for good in 1864.

Characteristics of the Vienna factory are: tea-pot spouts in the form of animal heads; handles in the form of the upper part of panthers, and human figures as covers for tureens. The porcelain is prized for its decoration rather than its shape, owing to the exceptional quality of its paintings: historical, Biblical and mythological scenes pictures by Vandyck, Titian, Rubens and Raphael, copied

F   [69]

from Vienna art galleries, are all depicted. There are also medallions in the style of Wedgwood, and copies of Japanese Arita. An attractive plate, of about 1820, was sold recently at Bonham's auction rooms in Knightsbridge for £2·50 (US $6). So we see that little fragments of this split-up grandeur have reached even as far as England today.

Ludwigsburg

A NOTE

Imitation, it is said, is the sincerest form of flattery. Ludwigsburg, like most of the smaller German factories of the eighteenth century, showed its appreciation by endeavouring to imitate Meissen. Duke Charles Eugène, with the help of his architect Hackher, opened his factory of Ludwigsburg in 1756, but his wares were inferior to those of most other German factories, being slightly greyish in colour. In spite of this, however, some of the figures of the rococo period are well modelled, as in the attractive example of fantasy work shown on this page.

After a courageous effort to stand up to the competition around it, the factory was forced to close down in 1824.

Nymphenburg

THE "SECRET"

In the middle of the eighteenth century a certain chemist called Härtl arrived in Nymphenburg, near Munich, where an unprecedented muddle over porcelain had been going on for some time. He wrote a book about porcelain with the unwieldy title of: *A Description of All Knowledge Appertaining to a Porcelain Factory in which by Means of Unceasing Industry and Many Experiments It was Brought to Fruition.* "Many experiments" were the operative words!

In 1729 a first attempt to make porcelain was tried in the neighbourhood of the Bavarian capital by a glassmaker called Elias Vater, who had arrived from Dresden offering the "secret". The Elector, Karl Albert, set aside 150 florins for a test and gave Vater in addition a weekly sum and free living quarters. But Vater's "secret", if indeed he had one, was unsuccessful. A further attempt at porcelain was made when the Elector married Anna Sophia, a granddaughter of Augustus the Strong, in 1747. She, like her grandfather, was interested in porcelain, and the Hall of Mirrors in the royal residence was completely decorated with tiles. Now a second "secret" appeared this time not from Dresden but from Vienna, conveyed by a certain Lippisch; but this second secret may have proved too heavy a burden for its owner who, before it could be tested out, either threw himself, or fell, into the River Isar.

A man named Franz Niedermayer then stated that he had the

Meissen "secret", which he had bought from a workman at an inn. This secret, however, proved to be no more than the half-knowledge which the Meissen workmen were in the habit of trying to sell to people for extra cash, behind their employers' backs.

Finally, the real "secret" arrived with Ringler, who insisted on carrying the precious information about with him everywhere in a great case. In this case, from which he was never parted, were plans for the kiln designs and directions for the mixing of colours. Perhaps this case proved too heavy for Ringler, for he only carried it for three or four years, after which his place was taken by the unwieldy writer on porcelain, Härtl. Härtl ran the factory with another director, Von Haimhausen, but when the Elector decided to move it from Neudeck to Nymphenburg in 1761, Härtl left, refusing to work at the new factory.

No wonder that at last the art of porcelain making flourished in the beautiful but artificial atmosphere with which it was surrounded at Nymphenburg. The factory was housed in a wing of the Palace, near to its famous Pavilion, one of the wonders of rococo art. An Italian stage designer had built a sort of Venice upon a sheet of water in front of the Palace. The pleasure-craft sailing on this was a kind of Armada galleon, with painted sails, rowed by eighty rowers with scarlet oars, and was used for theatrical entertainments by night, and fireworks displays for banquets after hunting parties. This seemed an appropriate setting for a young Swiss modeller from Lugano, Anton Bustelli, who had been working for the factory since 1754 and reached the climax of his fame at Nymphenburg. It is on Bustelli's work that the fame of the factory largely rests. Basically, as a modeller, he seemed to incline instinctively towards the theatre. His green huntsmen and ladies in riding-habits might be figures on the stage. His crinoline groups put one in mind of a Mozart opera. The dresses are plain-coloured instead of being flower-patterned, as at Meissen. Some of his works, however, seem to have been influenced by the mountain wood-carvers, especially when he leaves his figures uncoloured to show their shape and outline more distinctly.

Nowadays connoisseurs are beginning to show even more interest in Bustelli than in Kändler of Meissen, finding his work fresher and more original.

Nymphenburg's sponsor, Maximilian III, died in 1770, seven years after Bustelli's death, and was succeeded by Karl Theodor of the Palatinate, who owned a porcelain factory at Frankenthal. So, unfortunately, Nymphenburg found itself relegated to a second place. Also by 1780 the demand for German porcelain was lessening and cheap English earthenware, such as Wedgwood, was flooding the European markets.

Apart from Bustelli's work, Nymphenburg wares are competently painted, but follow the styles of Meissen. After 1770 we find birds and flowers and attractive landscapes, and the end of the century saw some work in the heavily gilded manner of Vienna. There were, however, some unusual animal subjects of horses being attacked by bears, and hounds fighting.

A speciality of the Nymphenburg factory was the *veilleuse* or *réchaud*, a foot-warmer in several parts heated by a small lamp. These were superbly painted and are now rare collector's pieces.

Some original types of decoration were used by this factory, such as lacework borders in gilt and pink and blue enamel, and an unusual floral effect was obtained from a design of maidenhair fern. There is also a very gay design called "Taffeta" or shot silk pattern.

Among the great small gems in porcelain are the Nymphenburg snuff-boxes and watch-stands in purple and gold.

In 1797 Frankenthal closed, and some of the Frankenthal artists came to Nymphenburg, which became a Bavarian State property till in 1862 it was leased to a private company, and as such it exists today.

Unfortunately, like the Meissen and Sèvres wares and many others of the eighteenth century, Nymphenburg wares are usually beyond the reach of any but the big collector. But though you may only be able to look at these tantalizing Bustelli figures through glass cases in museums, this in itself is rewarding enough. And, who knows? Sometimes, as Shakespeare wrote, "Fortune shows herself more kind than is her custom."

Delftware

THE FIRST CHARGER

When in the seventeenth century, the early English potters charged so courageously into earthenware, they started an industry which was to make English potters famous all over the world. Much experimenting amongst European chemists lay ahead before Western man was to enjoy the delights of his own manufactured porcelain in the eighteenth century. Porcelain, therefore, being practically non-existent in Europe, English Delftware workers, at their three main centres of Lambeth, Bristol and Liverpool, had less rivalry to compete with and their output was so great that luckily innumerable specimens of it are obtainable today.

How was it that these simple potters were able to learn such a complicated craft? They learnt it from potters from the Low Countries, Jaspar Andries and Jacob Jansen, who, as early as 1567, petitioned Queen Elizabeth for a patent.

The name "English Delft" is a misnomer and should not be mistaken for the Dutch Delftware. In reality a couple of generations of Englishmen were familiar with the process of making tin-glazed earthenware before they had probably even heard of Delft, nor did the town of Delft, in the middle of the sixteenth century, have a claim to fame. It is true that the English work was hardly to be compared with that of its relations on the Continent, namely Italian and Spanish maiolica ware, French and German faience, and Dutch

Delftware. The work was, however, characteristic of the homely vigour of the Englishman in the Stuart period, and one of its attractions to the collector today is the intimate way in which it brings him into touch with the domestic life of that time.

The ware was of soft earthenware, covered with a glaze of lead made opaque with an oxide of tin. On this white absorbent surface the decorator was forced to paint his pattern or picture very swiftly, as though he were working in watercolours.

The fame of the celebrated Blue-Dash Chargers, i.e., huge dishes, rests on the curious fact that their creators aimed at pure decoration at a time when they might have been expected to concentrate solely on objects of utility. We know this because on the back of some of the chargers there is a moulding for a wire cord, so that the charger, if not used for carrying a boar's head, could be hung on the wall.

They earned their name "blue-dash" because of the blue dashes, lines or dabs around the extreme outside edge. Their borders inside this were often of flowers, fruit and foliage, and they sometimes carried three spur marks in a triangular form on the face. Chargers are, unfortunately, museum pieces today, but plates, drug-jars, jugs, bowls, inkwells and candlesticks are in reasonable supply. For example, in London, in the sale columns of the Antique Collectors' Club, a Lambeth plate was offered recently for £11 (US $26), and a particularly attractive Bristol plate, decorated with peonies and an Oriental garden, was priced at £12 (US $29) in an antique supermarket; whilst a Liverpool bowl could be had at the same price in the Portobello Road, and a real bargain was a Delft inkwell at £4 (US $10) in Bermondsey Market.

The exuberance of the period found expression in the "Merry Man" series of plates. One, for instance, would have the inscription, "What is a Merry Man?" and another "Let him do what he can to entertain his Guests", followed by "With Wine and Merry Jests", and finally the warning: "But if his Wife do Frown, all Merriment goes Down". This reminds one a little of mottoes in crackers; but there are times when the plate speaks for itself, as:

On Me to Eat
Both Sauce and Meat.

English Delftware was immensely popular, and was very often made to order with the names and initials or arms of the purchaser. The plates, cups and mugs were prized in well-to-do households, special cups and jars being given as wedding-presents with the names of the bride and bridegroom inscribed on them. For less happy occasions the pretty apothecary drug-jars, often given away free, sweetened the pill of having to swallow medicine. It is a sobering thought that in those days a surgeon was not always forthcoming and the patient was forced to rely upon the tender services of the apothecary; so along with the drug-jars went bleeding-bowls. Such an apothecary was a Mr Battersby, a London friend of Pepys, who lived round the corner in Fenchurch Street, and as a leading apothecary had his jars inscribed with the names of drugs. The barber competed with the apothecary and had his bowls decorated with combs, scissors, soap, mirrors, shaving-brushes, razor-cases and razors. His bowls even had a piece cut out for the customer's head to rest in them.

Leaving aside the barber's and the apothecary's utensils, other popular objects were posset-pots, splendidly decorated, and caudle-cups for serving milk curdled with liquor. This beverage is described by a writer as "a furious and repellent liquid". Smaller items, obtainable today, are wine-labels and wine-cups. One of these cups had the National Anthem, as interpreted by the Jacobites, with the words, "*soon* to reign over us", as the Pretender was over the seas. Later, the

Whigs, adapting the word to the House of their Hanover patrons, changed "soon" to "long". The wine-pots were little fat vessels, hence the origin of the word "pot-bellied."

Around 1640 appeared wine-bottles based on Rhenish stoneware with inscriptions of wines such as "Whit", or "Sack"—the dry sherry that was Falstaff's undoing. John Tomes of Long Marston has his name on a Whit bottle of 1650. Perhaps Charles II, who took refuge in Tomes's House in 1651, after the Battle of Worcester, may have taken a swig from this very bottle.

As well as for cheerful drinking there was one amongst these wine-cups dedicated to sorrow. The Lambeth cuckold-cup of 1682, belonging to a certain I.M.F., bears this inscription: "Oi was Born to Wear the Horn", with a portrait of I.M.F., drowning his cares in drink.

Delftware takes us deep into the manners and customs of late Stuart and Georgian England. Like the American writer Alice Morse-Earle, who tells us, "How small was my knowledge of table manners till I discovered through my Delft how our ancestors ate", we can learn a lot about the customs of the times through studying earthenware.

Designs also tell us a great deal about the potters and their period. Some designs, as in most ceramics, were copied from the East, but in many of their other designs the potters show a quick-witted grasp of the changing times. Even their angels followed the fashion. The earlier angel was scanty-haired and puritanical, not unlike a nun. After the Restoration the angel acquired a fashionable wig. An angel of 1690 has a full William III wig and might almost be described as a winged portrait of the King. The angels are inclined to fade out with the century and to be replaced by fat cherubs, dragons, peacocks, songbirds, and baskets of flowers and fruit.

[79]

On the Blue-Dash Chargers are depicted men with the long and thick hair of the Stuart period, and this does not seem to vary whether the man be Adam, a king or a duke. A horseman will be riding at a fence, but Cromwell, for instance, is portrayed beside a church. The Old Pretender, unmistakably a Scotsman, has a Glengarry cap on his head, and many of the horses seem to be related to that ridden by Charles I, in the portrait by Van Dyck; but poor James II is both hatless and crownless, with his sash blowing out behind him as he gallops, obviously in great haste to escape.

In some designs pomegranate fruits frequently look like human faces. Adam can be of almost any nationality, such as an Eastern European gentleman, whilst Eve often looks as if she were Dutch. But these our first parents are usually not alone. The Garden of Eden is thronged with animals and the firmament is lighted with stars and moon as well as with the sun.

Outstanding in English Delftware are the blue and white landscapes and seascapes, the *chinoiseries* with which the Delft potters tried to stem the influx of imported Chinese porcelain, and, above all, the Blue-Dash Chargers; but at the end of the eighteenth century English Delftware was eclipsed by cheaper factory-made earthenwares.

Perhaps Horace Walpole does more than any other writer to join the period when Delftware flourished to modern times. Writing in 1783 about a Delft plate with a balloon design, he says: "Do not wonder that we do not entirely attend to things of the earth, fashion has ascended to a higher element. All our views are directed to the air. Balloons occupy philosophers, ladies, everybody . . .". Would that we had such craftsmen with us now, to depict man's triumphs on the moon!

Staffordshire Printed Earthenware

AS FRESH AS A DAISY

If you were to be so lucky as to fish a piece of Staffordshire printed earthenware, made in the early nineteenth century, from the bottom of the sea, the chances are that the design on it would be as clear as when it was first printed. By this printing process, at once so easy and economical, good designs were brought within the means of everyone, so this earthenware printed under the glaze, either in the more usual blue or in pink, green, black and other colours, became the staple crockery of the lower and middle classes throughout the nineteenth century.

The process was simple yet ingenious. The design was engraved on a copper plate, which was inked, and an impression taken on a piece of tissue-paper. This was then transferred to the piece of pottery to be decorated, and when covered by the glaze and re-fired would remain so firm that it could withstand the usage of time. It is not surprising, therefore, that there is no shortage of this printed earthenware knocking about today, for though most of it comes from Staffordshire, it was exported all over the world.

In England, printed earthenware is often the joy of the junk-shop hunter, for plates and dishes have a habit of turning up from the contents of old kitchen cupboards and store-rooms. However, when searching eagerly amongst a promising pile of these, the amateur would do well to remember that the potters would often pirate each other's patterns, so he should be wary in buying reprints of old wares, especially those on plates. The genuine old ware is lighter for its size than that made today and very often has three rough little marks round the rim, left by the "cockspurs" which the old potters used to keep their plates from sticking together when in the kilns.

The patterns were diverse. Many of them were illustrations from contemporary travel books, perhaps because in those days of the early nineteenth century it was difficult to get about and people may have used this ware as an early form of travel folder. There are copies of the Chinese K'ang Hsi blue and white, engravings of rustic scenes, beauty spots, cathedrals, ruins and harbours. Views were often framed in wreaths of flowers and foliage. The ware was not marked, but varying flower and fruit borders indicate to which factory the object could have belonged, such as Cheltenham and Harrogate with shell and flower borders, which were a favourite of Enoch Wood's, a well-known Staffordshire potter of the period. Ralph Stevenson of Cobridge specialized in English views with borders of acorn and oak-leaves, while Ralph Clews of Cobridge preferred cathedrals with bell-flowers. Thomas Mayer of Longport went in for vine-leaves and trumpet-flowers, Shelton for English churches with bell-flower borders, and Joseph Stubbs for American views with borders of eagles and flowers.

The trade with America also brought a host of American subjects. All the famous American personalities—Washington, Benjamin Franklin, etc.—were depicted, also American scenes such as Niagara Falls, as well as delightful reminders of old New York, Boston and Washington.

The best buys today are scenes of English country life with flower and fruit borders on plates, tea-sets and dinner-services. The collector may consider himself fortunate to be able to handle these objects and even in some cases, should it arise, to bite eighteenth-century soft-paste porcelain to test the glaze, for Simeon Shaw, writing in the early part of the nineteenth century, tells us that, in those days, "they were not to be pic'd, but took as they were put together".

After the 1840s special crockery was made for the nursery. The early examples set out to improve the children's morals; for instance, there would be a picture of a child offering his pocket-money to a beggar. It is small wonder that there are few of these left today, for if the child of those days was anything like his modern descendant, one can imagine him smashing such a "goody-goody" plate on the nursery floor. Presumably he did in some way rebel, for the factories soon stopped making this improving crockery and relented suffi-ciently to give the children nursery rhymes and stories for their pure pleasure. These can be obtained today.

For adults, humour was not lacking. Among the comic characters the most popular was Dr Syntax. This character was not unlike an English version of Don Quixote, always getting into trouble for the most chivalrous of reasons. The Doctor is often depicted as seated upon his horse named Grizel, who seems to have taken pleasure in overthrowing her master. This character was created by William Combe in a series of books written in 1812, entitled *Dr Syntax's Tour in Search of the Picturesque, Dr Syntax in Search of a Wife*, etc., and immortalized by Rowlandson's illustrations.

America, too, came in for its share of designs, after the War of American Independence. But here the Staffordshire potters were inclined to let their imaginations run riot. For example, there were plates representing Penn's Treaty, which was concluded with Indian tribes and signed under an elm-tree. But on the plates Penn is seen against a background of Chinese pagodas, himself dressed as a mandarin, holding the treaty in his hand, and the Indians, who must

[83]

have been war-stained and bedraggled, appear with beautiful head-dresses in fancy costumes, reminding one of a child's Red Indian set.

It was very often assumed that, because the process of printing on earthenware was so economical, it must lack artistry. A writer of the period was indeed very much concerned that the artists who created the designs were anonymous, for there was an idea that every name and every talent must be merged into the reputation of the factory. If a signature were there at all, it was, as likely as not, hidden timidly among the branches of a tree. Our writer deplored this modesty on the part of the designers by quoting the well-known couplet in Gray's *Elegy*:

> Full many a flower is born to blush unseen,
> And waste its sweetness on the desert air.

He would have been pleased to know that the "flowers" of Staffordshire earthenware are anything but wasted nowadays, and if for a moment they should chance to be "unseen", it is never for long.

Salt-glazed stoneware jug, 7½in/19cm high (£3; US $7); and a
nineteenth-century Doulton vase (£2; US $5)

Nineteenth-century Rockingham basket 7½in/19cm high

Mason's ironstone china plate, diameter 9¼in/23·5cm (£4; US $10)

Lustre Ware

POOR MAN'S SILVER

The word "lustre" means brightness or splendour. This seems appropriate, for its nickname of "poor man's gold" or "poor man's silver" fitted this ware that cheered many a cottage parlour in days when rooms were lit only by candlelight. In light or shade one lustre colour would often merge into another. A story is told of one collector who commissioned an artist to paint his lustre subjects in oils. The artist soon got himself into difficulties, for as fast as he painted one colour it changed into the next.

Before it became the homely "poor man's silver" this lustre ware had had a splendid ancestry. The Persians, who had an eye for the blending of colours, had produced lustrous pottery of great delicacy even before the thirteenth century. Wares of the same family turned up in Spain under the name of *Hispanomauro* about the middle of the fourteenth century, and Italy, in the sixteenth century, not to be out-done, added a brilliant ruby lustre glaze to its pottery. Finally England, at the end of the eighteenth century, rediscovered the lustre processes. It is not certain when the first pieces appeared, or who made them. They are seldom marked, as the big firms did not want their clients to think that they were running cheap lines; but lustre ware was made by nearly all the pottery firms, both large and small, and a good quantity of nineteenth-century lustre ware is obtainable today. Though still inexpensive, many authorities praise it highly,

G
[85]

and small collectors take pleasure in acquiring it, agreeing with a lustre authority, Dr Thorne, that "the best examples of pink and silver lustre are equal in artistic merit, if not in price, to Worcester and Crown Derby".

The pink lustre mentioned by Dr Thorne is derived from the purple of Cassius, invented by a Dutch chemist at the beginning of the seventeenth century, and dates, on lustre, from about 1810. But there are many varied groups of lustre ware, such as that wholly covered with plain metallic lustre to give the piece every appearance of gold, silver plate or beaten copper. A variation on this is "sprigged" with ornaments in relief. Another ingenious and much sought-after variety is the "resist" lustre, in which the lustre appears as a background to white or coloured patterns. Sometimes marble effects are obtained by mingling various tints. Lustre also lends itself to certain types of distinct figure-manufacture, such as the all-over lustre lions.

The collector need not limit his choice. He will find a wide range of jugs, mugs, tea-services, plates, etc., mostly with entertaining inscriptions and designs. Of jugs alone, there are many varieties. Puzzle jugs, for instance: a venture into rather heavy nineteenth-century humour, where the innocent drinker was the butt.

> Within this jug there is good liquor,
> 'Tis fit for Parson or for Vicar;
> But how to drink and not to spill
> Will try the utmost of your skill.

Another example of this humour at the expense of the customer might be a mug with a painted frog at the bottom.

Sporting jugs are also to be found, with incidents of the hunt; likewise farmyard scenes, naval and military heroes, such as a pirate on a ship or a seaman in a kilt. A very famous design on a jug was

Weymouth Bridge, opened in 1796, the largest single-span cast-iron bridge in the world, of which there were no less than twenty-eight different views.

Lustre, therefore, in its modest way, held a mirror up to history, as the enthusiastic American collector and author of the Victorian age, Alice Morse-Earle, tells us: "How vague were my school-days and my history lessons till I saw Lawrence of Decatur on a lustre jug, then I read eagerly every word of History." Just as this American girl learnt her history without tears on a jug, so, earlier, might a Regency girl have learnt hers. A historian of the times pilloried an unpopular monarch, George IV, who, according to him, "did more to lower the Monarchy in the eyes of the nation than any other King who has ever reigned"; and our Regency miss would have been able to read on a jug this inscription:

> When a man presumes to choose a wife
> He takes his lovely spouse for life;
> Who can judge and not repine
> The woeful case of Caroline.

So much for the jugs. The tea-services usually have a large and small bowl, the large being used in those days as a slop-basin and the small as a sugar-basin. It is curious that in the saucers of this lustre ware there is no depression to prevent the cup from slipping. A nineteenth-century writer comments on the point: "Years ago, having tea with an old lady, I noticed that she moistened the bottom of the cup with hot water to prevent it slipping in the saucer." The milk-jugs of the tea-services are often in the shape of a cow. Among the designs on lustre-ware plates are crudely painted views of houses, cottages, and churches, rather as if drawn by a child. Favourite designs to look for are strawberries in pink lustre with the leaves painted green, or Victorian children with their faces and arms in pink lustre, and their clothes painted in appropriate enamel colours.

Lustre mugs, besides sometimes having handles like dogs' heads, often bear sentimental engravings, such as those of Britannia weeping into a gargantuan pocket-handkerchief. These mugs were made to mourn the death of Princess Charlotte, who, as expected successor to her father, George IV, had been the great hope of the nation.

English sentiment at that time was outstandingly on the side of the Negro. Written on a mug we find, for example, this last couplet:

> Skins may differ, but affection
> Dwells in black and white the same.

Taxes seem to have been no more popular in those days than they are in ours:

> Success to the fleece, to the plough and the sail,
> May our taxes grow less, and our commerce ne'er fail.

Mugs also bore signs of the Zodiac, perhaps foreshadowing the magazine coverage of astrology today.

Who should wear the trousers has been an old ceramic joke down the ages, and lustre ware is no exception. On a mug we find:

> From rocks and sands
> And barren lands
> Kind fortune, keep me free;
> And from great guns
> And women's tongues
> Good Lord, deliver me!

This time the man seems to have got the upper hand!

A good deal of lustre ware was exported to America. Though the craze for it was as great as in Europe, one collector, John Spargo, seems to have qualified his enthusiasm: "People who do not know the charm of hobby-riding may think the hobbyist as cracked as some of my lustre pots". But one of America's greatest poets had no doubt about the lure of lustre ware. Longfellow writes:

> While the whole fabric is ablaze
> With varied tints all fused in one,
> Great mass of colour like a maze
> Of flowers illumined by the sun.

Salt-glazed Stoneware

A BREATH OF ENGLISH AIR

Our Victorian authority, Alice Morse-Earle, writing about a Staffordshire salt-glazed stoneware jug, says: "This old mottled stoneware jug, with the hound handle, stood in the deep shade of a stone wall, by the sunny side of a hayfield when first it met my view. It was filled with honest home-brewed beer for the haymakers. We sat watching them turn the fragrant hay until the beer had been drunk (and we did not have to wait long) and we bore the jug off in triumph, breathing to us forever the scent of new-mown hay with, to speak truthfully, a slight tinge of stale beer . . .".

This scene, though described by an American author, is as English as a painting by Constable and leaves no room for the intrusion of mandarins, pagodas or any other intriguing fantasies of the Orient. The English salt-glaze Staffordshire potters, refusing to rely, as most other European potters had done, on Oriental themes, were content to find their inspiration nearer home. To begin with they were indebted to the Germans, who discovered, in the fifteenth century, that if a hard earthenware is fired at a very high temperature it becomes semi-vitreous, non-porous, and sometimes semi-translucent; and further that if common salt is introduced into the kiln at a certain temperature, the result will be a dully lustrous, slightly pitted surface, resembling an orange-skin. So decorative was this that the Germans made wine-bottles of it and exported them to England as far back as the Elizabethan period. Later, in 1671, John Dwight, a London potter inspired by this work, obtained patents to make the same stoneware in England. The early German bottles were called Bellarmines, and bore a caricature mask of an unpopular cardinal of the times. Dwight, kinder to the English clergy, made no caricatures and his plain, brown or fawn-coloured jugs were without face-marks.

In the following century the English salt-glaze potters, carrying on Dwight's work, mixed in white clays which, by the middle of the century, burst into the full splendour of Staffordshire salt-glaze. "Splendour" is no exaggeration, because this new white surface imparted to the enamels a much greater brilliance than could be obtained on any other kind of body. Without sinking into the glaze the painting in enamel colours stood out with a jewel-like effect unequalled even on the finest porcelain. These glamorous objects, such as tea-pots and punch-bowls, command high prices today, when they can be found; but smaller objects such as toast-racks, money-boxes, butter-coolers, pudding and jelly moulds, fruit-dishes, pickle-trays, etc., are well worth looking for. Prices range from £3 to £30 (US $7 to $72), according to size. For example a tea-pot can be had for £28 (US $67), and a pickle-jar for £3.25 (US $8), in antique supermarkets. Easier to come by are objects in plain white undecorated stoneware.

The designs often have an English flavour, such as hunting scenes, Hogarth's Revels, crones and gaffers, drunken yokels and ploughing teams. If the proportions are sometimes at fault but the design pleasing, what matter if a hound is as big as a horse? The children depicted are often mischievous, such as a boy frightening a little girl by pulling an ugly face. The ware was practically indestructible and made a fortune for the potters, even finding its way into inns all over the Continent.

Unfortunately this salt-glazed stoneware suffered the same fate as other eighteenth-century hand-painted products, and by the early nineteenth century had been swallowed up by factory-manufactured articles.

The inventor, Dwight, more educated than the average potter, as he was an Oxford graduate, was bitterly disappointed because at first he thought he had discovered the secret of making porcelain. How near he was to it anyone can judge by a casual glance through the glass of many a famous collection, where a piece of painted Staffordshire salt-glaze seems almost to hold its own in brilliance of colour with that of Worcester or of Derby.

Plymouth and Bristol

THESE FLOWERS REMAIN

The thousand Sèvres porcelain flowers of Mme de Pompadour, the Chelsea flowers that banked London's dinner-tables—where are they today? A bunch or two survive in museums, but the majority have perished, like the natural blossoms they imitated. Only the porcelain flowers of Bristol remain, for the most part unbroken and unharmed, because they were once framed under convex glass in black pearwood frames.

This West Country enterprise had its source in a Plymouth chemist's interest in the Orient, and his determination to find out how the Chinese made their porcelain. William Cookworthy had been studying books about Chinese porcelain and he found china clay and china stone on the estate of his friend, Lord Canalford, in Cornwall. He experimented in a laboratory with friends in an attempt to make true porcelain out of this clay. His discovery created a revolution in the potter's art. He started a factory around 1768 at Plymouth. The works were at Coxside, where the buildings can still be seen, though they are now a shipwright's yard.

Cookworthy was a Quaker whose benevolence was greater than his dexterity. Many of the Plymouth and Bristol objects are clumsy and carelessly made, a fact which was to earn Cookworthy and his successors the animosity of Wedgwood. Though Cookworthy did not come of a potting family, he was not without drive, and he proved his determination to succeed by walking the whole way from Plymouth to London to find work to support his mother. He was to live to see the day when he could set her up as a hostess at her own table, where she entertained, amongst others, Captain Cook and Sweaton, the builder of the Eddystone lighthouse. A writer of the times describes Cookworthy thus: "I recollect his person very well. A tall, venerable man with a three-cornered hat and a bushy, curly wig, a mild but intellectual countenance, and full conversation." We learn also that "his eloquence in conversation was an intermitting flow of overwhelming oratory, but he would stop to answer the question of a child".

When the French Fleet appeared off Plymouth in 1779, Cookworthy was unable, as a Quaker, to take part in the fighting, but although well over seventy, he offered to take charge of the women and children and convey them to a place of safety. The centenary of his death in 1780 was commemorated in his native town in the following words: "This art has been cradled in our town, but the same town did not reward its gifted inventor and its spirited promoter as it should have done."

It does not seem to have done so, for we find Cookworthy obliged to sell out to Richard Champion in 1774.

The most famous Bristol wares were the biscuit-plaques: wreaths and garlands of natural flowers, usually round a portrait-bust or a coat-of-arms. These are not without their own interest, though they are museum pieces now. In one camellia alone we find no less than 57 separate petals, and in an anenome there are as many as 76 stamens. The figures also are now recognized as the most truly typical of English porcelain. A Bristol doctor is quoted as having said that he liked collecting Bristol figures of children, because the legs of the Bow children looked rickety, whereas the child figures of Champion looked healthy. In spite of this it has been said that the Bristol work lacked sensuousness; there is little richness of colour, only a cold hard glitter. For this reason, Bristol has sometimes been called the "Cinderella of ceramics".

Champion, for his part, does not seem to have been much more skilful than Cookworthy. There was a lack of control in his kilns which produced lopsidedness and distortion, so that objects which should have been similar, like mugs, were of different heights. Birds on Plymouth ware have enormously long necks and appear to be continually quarrelling. Some are frankly fantastic and some would-be natural, for they are often stiff and narrowly escape being caricatures.

The early blue was sometimes a cool grey, or occasionally a dark indigo. Ground colours which were rarely attempted, were mainly yellow or light blue.

Specialities of the factory which can still be found are jugs with masks under the lip, decorated with green-ribbon borders and bouquets of flowers; butter-boats; shell-shaped salt-cellars and ornamental shells; bell-shaped pint mugs and sweetmeat stands; cups and saucers plain in shape, with handles often askew through care-lessness; dishes like scallop-shells; pounce-pots (ie, used instead of blotting paper); ink-wells; and small trays.

Bristol has one unique characteristic: wreaths and festoons of laurel in green, interspersed with detached bouquets of flowers for tea-services. On the sauce-boats you will often find crudely drawn figures, male and female, in eighteenth-century country dress, against a sketchily drawn background. These are laboured copies from Chinese originals.

Champion's sloppy and careless work got him, as a successor of Cookworthy, into serious trouble with Wedgwood. This famous potter, usually so encouraging to anyone in his trade, poured scorn on Champion when he was in difficulties. One can only imagine that Wedgwood's dislike of amateurs incapable of controlling the shapes that they were potting caused him to write what was, for him, an unusually unkind letter: "Poor Champion, you may have heard, is quite demolished. It was never likely to be otherwise as he had neither professional knowledge, sufficient capital, nor scarcely any acquaintance with the materials he was working upon. I now propose to buy some growan-stone [ie, Champion stone] on easy terms."

Thus Wedgwood summed up the unfortunate business which caused Champion to lose all his capital and finally sell his patent for a pittance to a group of business men at New Hall. Nevertheless, some of the Plymouth and Bristol wares are far from being despised by collectors today.

Dutch Delftware

THE WINDMILL TURNS AROUND THE ORIENT

Long before the town of Delft had become famous for the making of tin-glazed earthenware, a type of Dutch Maiolica started by Italian potters who settled in Holland, had been made in the town as early as the fourteenth century. Unlike the English salt-glazed earthenware, however, Dutch Delftware takes its main inspiration from the Orient. Some of the earliest cargoes of that Oriental porcelain which was to become such a craze in Europe were shipped in Spanish galleons; but the homes of waiting Spanish grandees were unexpectedly robbed of these treasures by Dutch sailors who looted the galleons so proudly speeding to Spain. The Dutch potters were not slow to take advantage of such a precious windfall and thus laid the foundation of an industry that was to take its place among the great ceramic treasures of the world.

So accurate were the Dutch earthenware imitations of these Oriental porcelain models that, from a short distance, say behind glass in a cabinet, they are hardly to be distinguished from the Chinese originals themselves. This was indeed a remarkable feat, for the originals in blue and white were so exquisite that European lovers of beauty were inclined to worship them almost as thoroughly as they had been worshipped for centuries in the East. According to the words of an eighteenth-century Chinese poet, Chu Yen, the blue of this ware resembled the colour of the distant hills.

Blue as the sky, brilliant as a mirror,
Thin as paper, resonant as a musical stone.

Such was his description of this blue and white porcelain.

The dazzling whiteness of the glaze with its blue underglaze paintings of hitherto unknown Chinese figures and landscapes drew the eye irresistibly to any corner of the room where a piece was on display. No wonder was it, therefore, that with the acute scarcity of the Chinese originals, Dutch Delftware found its way even into royal homes. Such was the collection which William of Orange and Queen Mary brought with them to England and which can still be seen at Hampton Court. Some blue and white Delft tiles even graced the famous Pavilion de Faience, which Louis XIV built for Mme de Maintenon in 1670, but which unfortunately was destroyed in the nineteenth century.

By a curious coincidence the Delft brewing industry declined early in the seventeenth century, just when the fame of the Delftware potters was rapidly spreading. The potters then took over the breweries and bequeathed to their potteries some of the brewers' picturesque signs. When we read about the names, "Golden Flower Pot", "Four Roman Heroes", "Three Bells", "The Porcelain Bottle", "The Dutch Tankard", etc., we begin to wonder if we are reading about a Dutch pottery or an English pub.

It was not only the blue and white of the Orient that gave the Dutch potters their inspiration. The Chinese polychromes, that is to say porcelain which is painted over the glaze in enamel colours, were also copied. They include the *famille verte* of the K'ang Hsi period, made in the second half of the seventeenth century. This is usually a five-colour "palette", with green predominating.

Some designs were also a mixture of Chinese and European motifs such as Chinese figures against European buildings and *chinoiseries* that were fantasies on Oriental themes. These *chinoiseries* have been described as "China mania", for here the European artists tried to be more Chinese than the Chinese themselves.

On Dutch Delftware we also find copies of Meissen designs and European paintings, seascapes and Bible stories, as well as crude and amusing pictures of members of the House of Orange.

The range of objects is wide and various and, as the industry was so large and so many pieces were exported, there are a good many obtainable today. These objects include jugs, derived from the stoneware of the Rhine, tureens shaped like poultry or melons, tea-pots, coffee-pots, milk-jugs, sugar-basins, vinegar-stands, salt-cellars, pepper-castors, chemists' bottles, boxes for tobacco and snuff, square boxes for peat to keep the hands warm, boxes resembling prayer-books, bird-cages, plates on which were imprinted musical scores, which the guest could follow in song after a gay dinner-party, and even violins. There were also fan-shaped vases with tubular flower-holders for the famous Dutch tulips and, naturally, windmills.

It is possible to find examples of some of the more modest wares from £3 (US $7) upwards.

Unfortunately, the factories declined towards the end of the eighteenth century, being unable, like many other earthenware potteries, to stand up to the competition against Wedgwood's creamware. By 1790, there were only ten factories left, and by the early nineteenth century these had been reduced to two. The last factory closed down in 1820.

How are we to distinguish between original Dutch Delftware and the modern imitations which are flooding the markets today? The genuine soft earthenware body was rather vulnerable, thus examples showing no wear and tear are almost certainly fakes. Also true Delft often has a luminosity known to the potters as "flashing glaze".

[99]

As Père d'Entrecolles, the early eighteenth-century Jesuit mission-ary and authority on Chinese porcelain, tells us about the originals, and which might well be applied to Dutch Delfware, the ware appears "in all its beauty, almost in the same way as the natural heat of the sun makes the most beautiful butterflies, with all their tints, come out of their eggs".

Mason's Ironstone

THE HOUSEWIFE'S FRIEND

Having heard their mothers and grandmothers grumble about the late eighteenth-century china, which looked so lovely and broke so easily, the housewives of the early nineteenth century proved ideal customers for Charles James Mason's invention of ironstone china, when it appeared in 1813.

This ironstone china not only had the advantage of being as showy as the expensive bone china, which many could not afford to buy, but also lasted twice as long for, containing ironstone slag in its composition, it was almost unbreakable. Most of its decoration is pseudo-Oriental, in vivid blues, reds and greens.

Collectors of Mason's will probably find that this ironstone is cheaper today than many other kinds of earthenware. Prices range from about £2 (US $5) upwards, according to size. Some of the objects are unusually large, and these are mostly to be found in country sales: vases five feet high, for instance, mantelpieces, bed-posts, fitted basins and enormous tureens. Striking-looking jugs, some with dragon-handles, are very popular with collectors. For those who like the set-up of a Victorian bedroom, there are bedroom sets consisting of no fewer than eighteen pieces.

This successful invention naturally produced its imitators, but the genuine Mason-ware is usually marked with the name of the firm.

For those who are not afraid of the white elephants of the sale

H

rooms, outsize Mason objects can often be bought for the price of their carriage.

The blaze of colour which greets the eye from a Mason's plant-holder might almost be said to rival the glory of the flowers themselves.

Rockingham

THE EARL'S CHINA

It was the two earls of Rockingham who played an important part in the history of this factory, hence its name. The first earl, it is true, only played a minor role by renting his land to Yorkshire potters as early as 1757. This first earl is better known for his connection with pottery than for the fact that he was twice Prime Minister of England. Lecky, the historian, writes of him: "Of the new Minister there is little to be said. A young nobleman of very large fortune and un-blemished character, he had been for some time only remarkable for his passion for horse-racing." This earl, with his sporting tastes, was not likely to be a backer of culture, and it was left to his nephew, Earl Fitzwilliam, who inherited from his uncle, to be the great philanthropic supporter of the Brameld family who were to play the most important role in the development of Rockingham ware.

These Bramelds were artistic and talented, but their craving for perfection (they smashed all flawed wares and tossed them upon the discard heap) often led them into serious financial difficulties. Thus we find them bombarding Earl Fitzwilliam with begging letters on these lines: 'Your Lordship's feeling compassion for your fellow-creatures [is well known]. Upwards of fifty years of my life has been spent in anxious and persevering industry and I have gone grey with trying. It is not my wish to tire your Lordship with complaints but . . .". To which Lord Fitzwilliam's agent replied: "Lord Fitzwilliam is so peculiarly circumstanced this morning that he cannot get time to write." However, the earl relented in the end, and not a moment too soon, for the Bramelds were on the point of bankruptcy when at last, in 1826, the long wished for finance arrived.

Earl Fitzwilliam proved to be the ideal patron. He gave the potters a free hand to get on with their job, imposing no conditions. The potters, for their part, strove to justify his faith in them by creating some of the most outstanding porcelain of the period. One example of this is the Rhinoceros Vase (now to be seen in the Victoria and Albert Museum), surely the largest piece of porcelain in England, standing 44 inches (112 cm) high, with oak-branches entwined round a lion's paws and a rhinoceros on the top. As if this wasn't enough, the vase is also heavily ornamented with birds, flowers and scenes from the life of Don Quixote. Opinions of the period differ about this vase. John Ward, in his poem "The Potter's Art", writes:

> That splendid vase no vulgar hand designed,
> Its fabrick shews th' inventive Master-mind.

A more cynical writer, however, calls it "a nonsensical agglomeration", though the young Wordsworth seems to find it worth mentioning, for he writes: "[Musing] on a piece of china, I read the history of the errant-knight."

Amongst the simpler wares was a curious drinking-vessel called a "Sussex Pig", used at weddings in that county. The body forms the jug, and the head takes off. A toast of the time goes: "Will you drink a hog's head of beer to the bride's health?", proposed as the pig was being passed around.

Rockingham work became indeed so splendid-looking with its very elaborate decoration and gilding that it developed into a status-symbol of the period. The imagination of the Bramelds was boundless. Dinner-services were created with "Famous Houses of England" on the plates. About one of these, Creevy, a contemporary gossip-writer and gad-about, says: "I heard Princess Lieven say to Lord Fitzwilliam, 'Your house, my Lord, or your Palace, I should rather say, is the finest I have seen in England. It is both beautiful and magnificent. When foreigners have applied to me heretofore for information as to the houses best worth seeing in England, I have sent them to Blenheim . . . . But in future I shall tell them to go down to Wentworth where they can see all the most beautiful houses of England on dinner-plates.' " And when the Duchess of Cumberland ordered a Rockingham dinner-service of landscapes, she asked for "real views . . . none of your idealized romantic studies"; the idea being that guests, when dining, could be treated to a miniature picture-gallery. Writing in 1828, Ebenezer Rhodes says: "The study of botany has now become a tea-table amusement. A rose, a jasmine, a honeysuckle, the whole garden of Flora, is made to contribute to the ornamenting of this beautiful vase."

The Bramelds, not content with their English conquests, looked as far even as Russia in their hopes of finding the "deep purses" which they were forever seeking. But though they had the satisfaction of knowing that some of their tea-cups were set around the steaming samovars, the Russian nobleman proved, when it came to the reckoning, as loath to settle accounts as their English counterparts. The "deep purses", also, turned out to be a dream. Artistic glory but, alas, no corresponding financial gain! The artistic glory reached its climax when King William IV ordered a dinner-service. The Bramelds, as usual, regardless of expense, sent the service in a stout mahogany box rumbling off to Windsor, escorted by a squadron of cavalry.

No wonder expenses soared. Apart from reckless extravagance in production, wages were paid out to the most unsuitable people. For instance, a Chelsea Pensioner obtained "furlong" from the Chelsea

Hospital to work at Rockingham because he was reputed to be artistic; and William Cowan, who exhibited at the Royal Academy sixteen times, graciously accepted regular wages from the factory as a painter, even though he spent a great deal of his time on his own private work. So once again we find a begging letter from John Brameld: "The nervous anxiety of the writer is so great that he could not express himself personally, so he is sending his son to see you."

The Bramelds blamed everybody for their financial difficulties except themselves. There was the trade depression; the orders from Newcastle were not as good as they should have been "because the sad ravages of cholera have unsettled the state of men's minds so that they can no longer decide on china orders". Frantically they began to wonder if they could save the business by manufacturing something startlingly new. Four-poster beds were in fashion: why not manufacture porcelain bed-posts and curtain-rails? But by the time these objects were ready, four-poster beds had gone out of fashion and the Bramelds were left with these pretty but unsaleable pieces on their hands. A tip for collectors, for these bed-accessories are knocking about in junk-shops to this day.

By this time the long-suffering earl had had enough, and the Bramelds' last feeble attempt to exploit a new region by opening a pottery in Wales, which never materialized, failed to reconcile him. The pottery, after almost a hundred years' existence, was forced to close down in 1843.

Llewellynn Jewitt, who visited the site in 1870, writes: "Sad, desolate-looking wilderness; buildings altogether or half demolished. In the centre stands part of a building, the almost defaced words reading, 'This way to the China-Room'."

Today, after various ups and downs, including service as a smallpox hospital and a store-house, the great Waterloo kiln, one of the Bramelds' proudest follies, can still be seen above the roofs of the semi-detached houses. A ceramic enthusiast, after visiting the site in 1962, wrote: "In the coppice across the road, large trees had been blown down, among the exposed roots gleamed fragments of wares." A piece impressed "Brameld" the writer retained as a "forlorn souvenir".

But we can look for gayer souvenirs from Rockingham's great past, which included revived rococo, vases with three handles, painted decorations of flowers grouped in irregular patterns with brilliant, even garish colours, pieces liberally decorated with applied flowers, and views as topographically correct as could be achieved. Rockingham china feels substantial and has weight and solidity. The factory also specialized in cake-baskets with handles like criss-crossed twigs, castles and cottages as pastel-burners, shelters for night-lights, money-boxes, pipe-racks, inkpots, candlesticks, and the so-familiar "dogs" often to be found sitting on the mantelpiece of cottage-parlours today. It may be a far cry from the famous Rhinoceros Vase to the little cups and saucers, jugs, sugar-bowls, etc., but these objects are well worth looking for, and as the output of the factory was so prodigious, many of them have a chance of finding their way into a modest collector's cabinet.

[107]

Potlids

BEARS, SHRIMPS AND PACKAGES

Just as nowadays many firms attract the customer's attention to their goods by adding a little "something for free", so firms in the middle of the nineteenth century began to advertise their products, such as pomades, shrimps, conserves, etc., by multi-coloured potlids. These potlids were, in fact, an early form of selling goods by packaging design. Most of the early potlids were made by the firm of Felix Pratt and Co., of Fenton, Staffordshire. Each colour was separately fixed, the main colours being blue, green, yellow, orange and red.

Felix Pratt, himself, was fortunate in having with him an artist of the name of Jesse Austin. The two worked together for almost half a century, and Pratt, wearing a tall silk top-hat and driving his gig to work, and Austin, walking with a little limp, but also wearing a tall hat, became familiar figures in Fenton.

A man's fashion, rather than a woman's, helped to launch the business. Towards the end of the eighteenth century wigs were on their way out. Men began to take pride in their own hair and to lard it with a pomatum or bear's grease.

The bear motifs on potlids are some of Pratt's earliest designs. Some of them showed bears at play, or bears to whom human characteristics had been lent; for instance, there would be a bear reading a newspaper, studying at school or receiving a Valentine.

[108]

Some designs copied the writers who were inclined to sentimentalize bears, such as incidents from books by Seton Merriman, who wrote for children about the Rockies. Alas, poor Bruin! He was often to be seen in bear pits, or being tormented by hunters. These early bear potlids do not usually date after the middle of the nineteenth century, and are keenly sought by collectors today.

As well as the bear series there were pictures of topical English events, such as the Great Exhibition of 1851. The best of these bring vividly to life the Victorian scene, its heroes and heroines, everyday occupations, sports and pastimes. There were copies of pictures by famous artists, for instance, Gainsborough's "Blue Boy"; a very popular series was Shakespeare's "Seven Ages of Man".

Almost as popular, for selling shrimp and fish paste, was the Pegwell Bay series. The Bellevue Inn at Pegwell Bay had been visited by the Princess Victoria and her mother, the Duchess of Kent, in 1830. The young Princess must have been impressed by her visit, for later when she became Queen she gave the proprietor a Royal Appointment as "Purveyor of Shrimps and Potted Shrimps in Ordinary to Her Majesty". One wonders if the potlids had anything to do with this?

Many of these potlids are, unfortunately, being faked today. It is, however, possible to tell the genuine from the false, for the fakes have unconvincing colours, no "crazing" (ie, little cracks), and a quite different sort of "ring". When struck gently with a plate, the genuine lid will usually sound dead, while the false one, oddly enough will ring. How different from the result obtained by testing eighteenth-century glass!

The usual way, nowadays, to display a pretty potlid is to frame it in dark wood and hang it on the wall.

It is still possible to buy a potlid for about £3 (US $7) and upwards, but some are priced much higher.

Little did Pratt and Jesse, giving away their potlids so freely, imagine that in just under a century these same lids would grace the walls of many a fastidious collector.

Victorian China Fairings

"FOR JOHNNY'S SO LONG AT THE FAIR!"

> Oh, dear, what can the matter be?
> Johnny's so long at the Fair.
> (From a popular English folksong)

If you were strolling round a Victorian fairground in the years between 1860 and 1890, you would have seen, amongst the numerous wares on sale, small groups of gaily-coloured china figures made to catch the eye by their humour or sentimentality. These groups were known as "fairings". They were about $3\frac{1}{2}$ to $4\frac{1}{2}$ inches high and had plain, undecorated bases, with gilt sparingly used. Their colours were mainly shades of pink and blue, and they often bore a caption in black script.

No wonder our Johnny is so long at the fair! Besides hunting for his "bunch of blue ribbons", he will stop in front of each stall to examine its fairings before making his final choice of a present for his girl friend. He will have to make up his mind between a married couple having a difference: a husband being chastised with a slipper for having been out late drinking (it's doubtful if he'll choose this one!)—or, this is scarcely better, the doctor offering twins to a petrified husband: "Two little Beauties, aren't they?" says the caption. Johnny turns away. What have we here? A dentist at work: "A Strong Pull-Out, by Jingo!" He shudders.

Ah! this is better: a cat's tea party, one cat pouring out tea for the other. And this girl in a fanciful dress and hat with floating ribbons, so unsuitably clad to be "Waiting for The Bus". That might be a good joke! Or here is a girl, riding a bicycle, complete with bustle, little hat and short boots. But already this has been snapped up, for it is the latest craze.

Our Johnny will linger long for, apart from these simple themes, there are others that he will not understand so well and that will take him a little time to puzzle out. There are also some which make him a little sad. These boot-blacks, chimney-sweeps, and boys selling newspapers or matches. These pathetic figures have certainly been designed with a purpose; they might have stepped straight out of one of Dickens's books. Then there are the English nurses who are impartially looking after the soldiers of both sides in the Franco-Prussian War, thus trying to prove that England has been right to maintain her neutrality. A gayer note is struck by Champagne Charlie, a popular music-hall character, and the American actor, Edward Sothern, who introduced Dundreary whiskers to the "mashers" of Victorian England.

Fairings were so popular amongst the Johnnies of the period that the English manufacturers were forced to enlist the aid of a German firm called Elbogen, whose fairings, marked with their name, are equal in value to the English ones. If the Johnny of the present day wishes to make a nice gift of a fairing, something really pretty, or humorous, he will only have to spend, say, from £3 to £5 (US $7 to $12) on such an offering. He will find everything that could be had at a Victorian fair in junk-shops or in street markets.

But . . . "Oh, dear, what can the matter be?" For not only Victorian fairings but the whole fascinating range of porcelain and earthenware, from eighteenth-century Worcester and Derby, through Spode and Delft, down to potlids, are his to choose from today. No wonder he is "so long at the fair"!

Conclusion

Having, as we hope, encouraged you to go porcelain hunting, we wish you good luck in your quest for "These Minor Monuments", and give you a few tips to help you on your way.

As concerns luck, there is a superstition amongst some English street-market traders that if they make their first sale of the morning before they have finished unwrapping their wares, they will get good prices for the rest of the day. This superstition sometimes makes them prepared to sacrifice their profit and part with an object for scarcely more than its purchase price. Here it is the early bird that catches the worm, even as early as 5.30 a.m., at Bermondsey Market! But don't let the hour shock you; you will be in good company. It's quite the thing amongst bowler-hatters now to give themselves a little pre-weekend treat on Friday mornings. Visitors to London from overseas are also beginning to look upon Bermondsey Market as a treasure trove.

We all know how easy it is to lose keys. Therefore it is not surprising that pieces of furniture which have been knocking about for a hundred years or so should have locked drawers. The careful examiner at a sale preview will often come across such a drawer. If the object is not too heavy, he can shake it, and a rattle may betray that there is something inside. Such "pig in a poke" buying is necessarily a gamble, but, who knows? The rattling sound may turn out to be a miniature, or a delicious Battersea enamel box.

In any buying at auction sales, in junk-shops or on street markets, somebody has to make a profit, however small. This is where the members of the Antique Collectors' Club, at Clopton, Woodbridge, Suffolk, have a distinct advantage in being able to make person to person sales. The club takes no percentage between buyer and seller, but supports itself entirely on its membership fees. It is exclusive to collectors, one of its rules being that no dealer may join.

Even in helping others you may sometimes help yourself. Collectors' pieces have been known to find their way into Oxfam shops, Church bazaars and jumble sales. It is all rather like a lucky-dip in a bran-tub, but when old houses are dismantled and drawerfuls of stuff are given away, who knows what may turn up?

Finally, bidding in the middle of the day at auction sales can be hungry business and dealers, once they have got what they came for, are apt to go off and have a good lunch. With the dealer out of the way, the more enduring amateur has the chance of picking up a real bargain amongst the later lots. So, good hunting!

FOR FURTHER READING

Aldridge, Eileen *Porcelain*. London: Paul Hamlyn, 1969

Bedford, John *Looking in Junk Shops*. London: Max Parrish, 1961; New York: David McKay, 1964

Bemrose, Geoffrey *Nineteenth Century English Pottery and Porcelain*. London. Faber, 1952

Bemrose, William *Bow, Chelsea and Derby Porcelain*. London: Bemrose, 1898

Church, Sir Arthur H. *English Porcelain*. London: Chapman and Hall, 1911

Cushion, J. P. *English China Collecting for Amateurs*. London: Muller, 1967; New York: Barnes and Noble, 1967

Cushion, J. P. *Pocket Book of (English) (French and Italian) (German) Ceramic Marks*. London, Faber: 1961 to 1965; Boston: Boston Books, 1965

Dixon, J. L. *English Porcelain of the Eighteenth Century*. London: Faber, 1952

Fisher, Stanley W. *English Blue and White Porcelain of the Eighteenth Century*. London: Batsford, 1950

Godden, G. *British Pottery and Porcelain 1780–1850*. London: Arthur Barker, 1963

Hayden, Arthur *Chats on English China*. London: Ernest Benn, 2nd ed. 1952

King, William *English Porcelain Figures of the Eighteenth Century*. London: Medici Society, 1925

Nightingale, J. E. *Contributions Towards the History of Early English Porcelain*. Salisbury: Bennett Bros, 1881

Reynolds, Ernest *Collecting Victorian Porcelain*. London: Arco, 1952

Savage, George *Eighteenth Century English Porcelain*. London: new ed. Spring Books, 1964

Savage, George *English Pottery and Porcelain*. London: Oldbourne Press, 1961

Thorpe, W. A. *Porcelain as an Art*. London: Harrap, 1932